Studying New Zealand

A Guide to Sources

G.A. WOOD

University of Otago Press

Published by University of Otago Press,
PO Box 56/56 Union Street, Dunedin
Fax: 64 3 479 8385
Email: university.press@stonebow.otago.ac.nz

Printed by GP Print Ltd, Wellington

Cover images are from *Official Catalogue and Souvenir of the New Zealand
International Exhibition, 1906–1907.*

Contents

Preface

This guide to sources draws upon years of immeasurable assistance from librarians and archivists. For this edition I am particularly indebted to Elizabeth Tinker and Sheila Williams. The guide has been reorganised along lines suggested by Jim Traue, preliminary revision work was undertaken by Ellen Ellis, and the chapter on finding Maori information was written by Kirsten Stewart.

Without this help this revised edition would not have been possible, or at any rate it certainly would have been less complete and more error prone.

G. A. Wood,
December 1998

1. Studying New Zealand

1.1 Studying New Zealand

Beyond books has come the computer. Printing gave the means of the few communicating to the many. It was one-way communication. Computers not only open the storehouse of printed materials to all — or at least to all who can afford or have access to modern technology. They revived and extended information exchange. 'The earliest system for storing information and transmitting it from one person to another was language'. By word of mouth 'history, rituals, stories, prayers, and medical and other knowledge were passed on from one generation to another'.[1] The computer has made person-to-person interaction the basis not just for passing information from generation to generation but also from continent to continent.

In studying a society we look both to the most advanced information systems, and to the oldest and most established: language, drawings, song and dance. Missionaries brought the written word to New Zealand. The language was codified, captured in writing (cf. *Book & Print in New Zealand,* edited by Penny Griffith and others, 1997 [noted below **4.9**]): rituals, customs and traditions and scientific knowledge of the New Zealand people came to be stored in cold print, some of which is now re-emerging in modern publication, such as *Nga Korero A Pita Kapiti: the teachings of Pita Kapiti,* translated, edited and annotated by Anaru Reedy, Christchurch, 1997. This could not end the importance of oral tradition; indeed recognition of the importance of oral history has grown as efforts are made to record on tape and in written testimony traditions and recollections from the country's past. Interest has grown enormously with recordings being used now for such purposes as evidence before the Waitangi Tribunal. Where once, in the quite recent past, historians might view with suspicion the 'anecdotal nature' of oral history, now it is widely used as a research tool in a variety of disciplines. Oral history has been used to come to better understanding of the unique New Zealand mix of cultures, especially the mix of the two peoples, tangata whenua and tangata tiriti. Through genealogy and oral tradition history is stretched

---

1 Jean Key Gates, *Guide to the Use of Libraries and Information Sources,* 7th edition, New York, 1994, p. 3.

back well before the advent of written records, adding to what can be learnt from such techniques as carbon dating. Oral tradition, too, can be drawn upon to interpret the messages contained in the drawings, carvings and other artefacts with which peoples have expressed and developed their culture.

This work seeks not to examine all the various dimensions of studying New Zealand, but to provide a guide to the sources of studying. Digging, listening, or watching are means of obtaining information; this work tries to describe how one may access the information that has been obtained. Through the world-wide network of computers, the Internet, as those familiar with it well appreciate, there is ready unfolding of sources after initial access is achieved: the focus of the following pages is more on other, and more traditional, sources. Given the rapidity with which material is being computerised, however, the researcher should be aware that many traditional information sources are also accessible on the Internet, if not today, then by tomorrow.

An obvious place to start checking sources is in the public book collection. Even before setting out there, however, it is helpful to study some brief map of terrain intended to be traversed. One wants to find books, articles, essays, which give a broad overview. How?

In 1993 the National Library produced the slim *Working Titles: Books that shaped New Zealand* edited by Susan Bartel, Wellington, to accompany an exhibition. More comprehensive used to be a section in the annual *New Zealand Official Yearbook* [cited below **4.10**] which included a select bibliography of New Zealand books, for the guidance of both New Zealanders and overseas readers. Unfortunately there is no substitute today for that listing — although there is a modern informative work that sticks to its lathe as a straight compilation of statistics and basic information: David C. Thorns and Charles P. Sedgwick, *Understanding Aotearoa/New Zealand: Historical Statistics*, Palmerston North, 1997 [**4.12**]. To our benefit, of course, an ever burgeoning number of books being published has made well-nigh impossible the task of presenting a simple list of basic texts or key works.

It is possible, however, to indicate some routes and some guides to direction which provide the bases for modern information services for the researcher and writer.

1.2 New Zealand yesterday and today

Through New Zealand's time of European settlement writers have tried to describe the country to outsiders: from works such as John Savage's *Some Account of New Zealand: particularly the Bay of Islands and surrounding country; with a description of the religion and government, language, arts, manufactures, manners and customs of the natives, &c. &c.*, first published 1807 (reprinted in facsimile 1966, 1973), to F. L. W. Wood's *Understanding New Zealand*, New York, 1944, for war-time United States. Today the focus is on the domestic reader. Wood's book, for example, later appeared in various editions in revised format as *This New Zealand,* 1946-1958. A work of the 1990s which endeavours to give an overview of the society is *The New Zealand Society A Sociological Introduction*, edited by Paul Spoonley, David Pearson, and Ian Shirley, Palmerston North, 2nd ed., 1994. Its twenty chapters range through such topics as 'family', 'social policy', 'work', 'religion'. From a different perspective is *The Political Economy of New Zealand*, edited by Chris Rudd and Brian Roper, Auckland, 1997, which is intended to review New Zealand's economy, its civil society and the state in the postwar era. For what might be called 'pulse-taking' — how insiders see New Zealand on a day-to-day, or year-to-year basis — two long-standing journals of comment stand out: *Landfall*, 1947–, semiannual since 1993 (previously quarterly), and the weekly *New Zealand Listener*, 1939–. Today they are joined by such glossy yet substantial magazines as the monthly *North and South*, 1986–.

Standard histories of New Zealand are Keith Sinclair's paperback *A History of New Zealand*, latest edition Auckland, 1991, and *The Oxford History of New Zealand Second Edition*, ed. G. W. Rice, Auckland, 1992. But in some ways creative writing, unbound by requirements of scholarly justification and formal referencing, may better convey the culture of a society than the academic text produced for scholars and students. Oxford University Press has also produced the key introduction to New Zealand writing: *Oxford History of New Zealand Literature in English*, ed. Terry Sturm, 2nd ed., Auckland, 1998 [cf. **4.9** below].

Oxford is the publisher, also, of *An Anthology of New Zealand Poetry in English*, ed. Jenny Bornholdt, Gregory O'Brien and Mark Williams, Auckland, 1997: 'nothing short of brilliant', one reviewer wrote of this 500-page collection of poems by over one hundred New Zealand poets; it gives New Zealanders the possibility of seeing where we are, where we were and where we might be.[1] With different focus is *Lake, Mountain, Tree; An Anthology of Writing on New Zealand Nature and Landscape*, edited by Philip Temple, 1998.

Biography and autobiography also offer a rich resource for understanding both the past and the present. Victorian England produced scores of two-volume 'Lives and Letters' of leading public figures, and modern British notables bettered this by writing up their own accounts of their lives and times, drawing perhaps on state archives as well as on their own private records and journals. Until recently, however, New Zealand public figures have left comparatively little in the way of published writings. William Gisborne, Alfred

---

1 Hamish Wyatt, in *Otago Daily Times*, 8 Feb., 1997

Saunders, W. P. Reeves, John A. Lee, Sir John Marshall, and Sir Robert Muldoon may be cited as exceptions to a general rule. There was, however, a succession of works by acute observers, locals and visitors, which are both useful and readable: A. S. Thomson, F. E. Maning, Anthony Trollope, C. W. Dilke, and André Siegfried are notable examples. In this category, too, could be included descriptions of their contemporary society by New Zealand historians such as Sir Keith Sinclair (for example in the concluding pages of the various editions of his Penguin *History of New Zealand*) or F. L. W. Wood, in the changing portrayals of New Zealand given in the different editions of *This New Zealand* (1944 to 1958).

The richness of a society is seen most obviously perhaps in its visual arts, its buildings, carvings, paintings, photographs. The still **photograph** covers almost the entire period of European settlement: Lieutenant-Governor Eyre brought a camera with him to New Zealand in 1848. There is a history by Hardwicke Knight, *Photography in New Zealand: a social and technical history*, Dunedin, 1971, and *New Zealand Photography from the 1840s to the present*, by William Main and John B. Turner, Auckland, 1993, gives quick references to over eighty photographers. On Wellington photographers there is William Main's *Wellington Album*, 1998. Hardwicke Knight and William Main between them have in fact produced a number of publications on New Zealand photography and New Zealand photographers. The New Zealand Centre for Photography in Wellington produces the *NZ Journal of Photography*, 1992– (formerly its *Newsletter*). A wide-ranging pictorial record of New Zealand's past is provided by popular weeklies of which two leading examples survived until the age of television: the *New Zealand Free Lance* (1900-1960) and the *Weekly News*, Auckland (under various titles from the nineteenth century until 1964). Phillip Ridge and Stephen Barnett between them have compiled a series of volumes covering 1900 to 1970, decade by decade (or two decades, for 1900-1919): *Those Were The Days: a nostalgic look at the early days ... from the pages of the Weekly News*, Auckland, 1987-89. There is also an *Index to Maori photographs in the Auckland Weekly News, 1898-1924*, Auckland, n.d. Another weekly, valuable for its photographs in its later decades, was the *Otago Witness* (1851-1932).

Gordon H. Brown has produced *Visions of New Zealand: Artists in a New Land*, Auckland, 1988, with 190 illustrations which show how nineteenth-century New Zealand was seen through the eyes of artists — amateurs and professionals. Some indication of the wealth of New Zealand's historical **paintings** also is given by the handsome illustrations — over 5,000 — in *New Zealand's Heritage: The Making of a Nation*, 1977-79 [cf. below **4.2**]: a list of artists is included in the index.

New Zealand **museums** have developed extensive collections of Maori artefacts, although zealous collectors of the nineteenth century transferred many items of the New Zealand heritage to institutions or private hands overseas. Conversely, of course, there are significant representations of the European, Asian and Oceanic cultural heritage held in New Zealand.

One can, as it were, walk into New Zealand society at Te Papa Tongarewa, the Museum of New Zealand (MONZ): one of the most exciting responses of recent times to desire to learn more about society and the environment. Te Papa reflects New Zealanders' high level of interest in culture and cultural activities — revealed for example in a July 1997 survey conducted by the Ministry of Cultural Affairs. It absorbed the National Art Gallery along with the National Museum into an innovative and interactive experience for visitors to 'our place', Te Papa. But Te Papa caps, not supersedes, the strength of regional and district institutions through New Zealand. Together with the better-known major provincial museums and galleries there is a host of small local and specialist collections — totalling approximately 600 all told through New Zealand, and including such as the New Zealand Cricket Museum, housed in a leaking building in Wellington.

Keith W. Thomson, *A Guide to Art Galleries and Museums of New Zealand*, Auckland, 1991, is an attractive directory, excellent for tourists. Some museums also produce their own guides, such as the *Visitor's Guide to the Museums of Otago and Southland* produced by the Otago Museum, 1988. There is a *New Zealand Museums Journal: journal of the Art Galleries and Museums Association of New Zealand*, Palmerston North, 1991– (continuing an earlier *Agmanz Journal*), and Creative New Zealand brought out a statistical publication, *New Zealand Museums 1990-96: facts and trends*, 1997. There was a museums address list produced by the Museums Association, updated in 1998 as *The Directory of New Zealand Museums*, edited by Tony Cairns, Wellington.

2. The Electronic Age

2.1 Computer talk
2.2 Online databases

2.1 Computer talk

A computer connected to the Internet is connected to a world of almost infinite expanse of knowledge and amusement.

The Internet began as a communications system for the United States military in the 1960s, and the linking by phone of computers at military sites and some large universities. With increasing rapidity, it has spread to become the global information highway, although only in the 1990s did it become — as one author puts it — 'sufficiently robust and user-friendly to make networking an effective means of communication, as well as an information exchange, for the general public'.[1] In a decade, from 1987 to the 1997, the number of hosts on the Internet grew from 20,000 to 20,000,000. Through the Internet, the so called network of networks, computers can 'talk' to each other over a phone line. They can use any language, of course, but — reflecting its origins — English is the official language of the Internet, to the tremendous advantage of most New Zealanders.

Through libraries, institutions' networks, cyber or internet cafés, anywhere around the world, it is possible to access the Internet. New Zealand has a rapidly increasing and high percentage of households with personal computers: the Internet can be accessed also from home through an Internet service provider. There are more than fifty providers in New Zealand. All the researcher needs is to have a computer connected to the telephone system (through a modem attached to, or inside the computer) and the services and software of the Internet service provider. For those who can afford a computer, the charges for Internet service are not heavy: they cover joining/connection fee, a monthly rate and/or charges by the minute when online and using the Internet. (There is a bias towards income and education in Internet users: as commentators observe, as Internet use continues to spread and the Internet becomes a critical tool for information and communication, ever widening the gap between the

---

1   *Words have Wings. Teaching and Learning with Computer Networks*, edited by Kwok-Wing Lai, Dunedin, 1996, p.1

info-rich and the info-poor, 'the political issue of who can afford access will become increasingly important'.[1])

Once connected the researcher can use e-mail (electronic mail), access the World Wide Web and join various discussion groups. Chances are that in any field a researcher will find some group happy to exchange comments and information in that area of specialisation. In journalists' clichés: in the most revolutionary technological breakthrough since the 15th century, the global village is shrinking while its library is expanding — explosively.

Much time can be spent (and much time wasted) surfing the Internet. Internet service providers give all the basic guidance necessary to get online. To fully exploit the Internet — and for learning something about it generally — there are a number of publications available, for example the local D. Merritt and P. Reynolds, *Internet: A New Zealand User's Guide,* Auckland, 1995, Peter Wiggin, *Wired Kiwis: Every New Zealander's Guide to the Internet*, Christchurch, 1996, and R. W. Wiggins, *The Internet for Everyone: A Guide for Users and Providers*, New York, 1995. Note, however, the publication dates of these guides.

Beginners might prefer to start with *The Internet for Dummies*, by John R. Levine, Foster City, 1997, a work which is as its name implies. Also written for absolute beginners — including explaining the meaning of such mysteries as 'http' (Hypertext Transfer Protocol) — and itself on the Internet is '*Exploring the World Wide Web*' (http://www.gactr.uga.edu/exploring/index.html) from the University of Georgia. '*Learn the Net — An Internet Guide and Tutorial*' [www.learnthenet.com/english/index.html] is a comprehensive guide which includes good coverage on how to do effective web searches. The enthusiast will find various other guides on the Internet — as well as being able to subscribe to such publications as *New Zealand NetGuide* (produced eleven times a year, www.netguide.co.nz). Access is becoming progressively simpler, especially with development of technology to link the Internet with a standard television set.

As experienced surfers suggest, however, researchers starting out could adapt the scientists' rule of thumb, 'when all else fails read the instructions', to: 'when all else fails ask a librarian or someone who knows'.

Software is available which can search library catalogues across the Internet for research materials and books. Through search engines such as Yahoo!, HotBot or AltaVista the World Wide Web can be explored for information and networks on any and all topics.[2] Increasingly organisations have their own websites, giving contact points, access information, guides to best sites, news stories, press

---

1   cf. Warren Caragata, *Maclean's*, November 23, 1998, p.104.
2   See Laura.B.Cohen, 'Searching for Quality on the Internet', *Choice* Suppl.35.

releases and new information — such as official reports for government agencies — catalogues of publications, and in some cases even providing for interaction. The 1998 white paper on tertiary education, for example, was published by the Ministry of Education on its website, www.minedu.govt.nz/Tertiary/Review/. Reports of the Waitangi Tribunal can be found [www.knowledge-basket.co.nz/waitangi/welcome.html].

GLOBE (Global On-line Business Enterprises) has produced comprehensive directories of websites in a number of countries, including New Zealand [www.peg.apc.org/~globenz/index.html].This is probably as convenient a means as any to find different libraries, for example.

2.2 Electronic databases

Through the Internet an individual would appear to be able to have free access to a surfeit of information; however there is much more still that is available, but on a cost basis. For example, the New Zealand Bibliographic Network — now Te Puna — (on which were to be found items of the New Zealand National Bibliography) [below **5.1.1**] normally could be accessed only through a subscribing library. And there is a great range of other databases and networks. The annual *Gale Directory of Databases*, Detroit, has information on more than 10,000 databases. Although using them costs money, and the information contained in them does not usually reach back very far into the past, they can save the researcher hours of manual searching and they provide access to a resource pool larger than any individual library can provide. An excellent printed work is the very substantial annual *Information Industry Directory: an International Guide to Organizations, Systems, and Services Involved in the Production and Distribution of Information in Electronic Form*, Detroit, New York, Toronto, London.

What has been published? Where? Where in New Zealand can copies be found? There is ANZBiP online, produced by RMIT Publishing with D. W. Thorpe, listing 120,000 in-print and out-of-print Australian and New Zealand books, and the annual printed *New Zealand Books in Print* including all series available in New Zealand as well as books, and there are several sites on the Internet through which current publications can be identified and, more importantly for the researcher, both local and overseas bibliographic databases can be accessed. For older works there are various databases as well as the traditional range of printed guides [see **Bibliographies, 5.**, below].

At the close of the 1990s, and with Y2K (year 2000) looming, the National Library was forced to replace its ageing computer systems which were using technology developed in the 1970s. In 1999, the millions of electronic bibliographic references and documents held in the National Library were moved to the new computer system.

The national bibliographic service from 1999 is Te Puna, listing publications, including those not held in New Zealand, and indicating New Zealand libraries' holdings. Te Puna replaced and provided similar services to the New Zealand Bibliographic Network, phased out 1998-1999. It is a network linking most public, university and government department libraries with the National Library in Wellington. The network contains bibliographic information on many million books and journals, updated every week with information on new publications from the United States, Britain, Canada and Australia, as well as new New Zealand material. Gradually, too, older material has been added to the database.

From 1987 the New Zealand National Library's Kiwinet had offered bibliographic and full-text New Zealand databases but, following a review of Kiwinet, the National Library ceased hosting externally-sourced databases from the end of 1997. Some databases formerly on Kiwinet subsequently were provided by Status Publishing Ltd [www.status.co.nz], including a number of newspapers produced by Independent Newspapers, such as the *Dominion* and *Evening Post*, from January 1995, *Sunday Star-Times*, from December 1995, *The Press*, from June 1996 (— note that some newspapers are available gratis on the Internet). Principally Status Publishing Ltd is a vendor of databases on New Zealand law: statutes, regulations, court judgements.

Status is available through

- the Knowledge Basket — New Zealand, http://www.knowledge-basket.co.nz/

This vendor offers a range of databases including New Zealand Science (formerly STIX — aka SIRIS) [**4.11**], legal databases (LINX), case law on Briefcase, Brookers, and legislative information (GP Legislative), company information (DATEX), and indexes to newspapers (Newspaper Index) and business publications (Newzindex).

A good directory of New Zealand databases is Lincoln University Library's

- Ara Nui — Many paths

which, as it affirms, 'will guide you to internet sources of Aotearoa/New Zealand information, World Wide Web sites, Telnet sites, and Usenet newsgroups included': http://www.lincoln.ac.nz/libr/nz/ is one of the most convenient sites from which to start a search.

Many of the large **international** databases are now also available on CD-ROMs (Compact Disc–Read Only Memory) which are regularly updated; hence it is possible for a library to hold data in-house. The CD-ROM business is indeed booming: a Microsoft catalogue of 'Essentials for Work and Play' for home use, for example, lists a comprehensive *Encarta Reference Suite* of encyclopedia, atlas, and dictionaries—a strikingly impressive reference tool available at quite modest price for what it contains. (On the Internet: www.microsoft.co.nz.) *Global Books in Print*, Bowker Electronic Publishing 1994–, on CD-ROM, has, 'complete English-language bibliographic information from the United States, United Kingdom, continental Europe, Australia, New Zealand, Africa, Asia, Latin America, Canada, and the Oceanic states' and includes a subject guide and forthcoming books.

Beyond the written word is access to the **pictorial**. With computer imaging technology the Alexander Turnbull Library's Image Services, for example, is transforming masses of its vast collection into digital data, which can be reproduced in a variety of high-quality formats. On the Internet through Timeframes searchers can search, download, and order heritage images from the Library collection, either printed or digital [http://timeframes.natlib.govt.nz]. Online images include photographs, drawings, prints, paintings, posters, cartoons, maps and manuscripts — and the Timeframes database grows daily, expected to total 20,000 images by the year 2000.

Electronic media open a vast information storehouse, with well-signposted aisles, cross-connections and intriguing nooks. Increasingly the researcher and writer can travel the world and explore its information resources without moving from a desk. And yet — to explore the New Zealand of past and present, it is still to the traditional forms of recording that the researcher must also turn for sustained discussion or for occasions for prolonged contemplation, to join artists, writers, composers and others in posing questions, in grappling with issues, in self-expression, in recording, or simply in laughter and distress.

3. Libraries and Research Collections

3.1 Libraries and research collections

Rich as may be the resources of New Zealand's many public and university libraries, the researcher quickly becomes aware of the need to turn to various specialist libraries, including in some cases libraries overseas [cf **5.1**: National bibliographies, and **Archives and manuscripts**: **9.7**.] Thanks to the Internet a wide range of library resources and much of individual library catalogues can be accessed electronically. Nevertheless, the Wellingtonian is particularly well placed, with such centrally located capital city facilities as the National Library and especially its separate Alexander Turnbull Library, the National Archives [**9.3**] (which also has offices in Auckland, Christchurch and Dunedin), Te Papa, the Museum of New Zealand [already mentioned above **1.1**], and the Parliamentary Library. Facilitating use of Wellington's research resources at the city's Victoria University is the interdisciplinary Stout Research Centre for the Study of New Zealand Society, History and Culture, which was established in 1984. Membership of the Centre is open to all interested persons. The Centre sponsors seminars and conferences and provides study facilities for visiting scholars. Victoria University of Wellington also hosts the Centre for Strategic Studies and the Institute of Policy Studies.

Beyond Wellington's well known national research collections is a host of smaller ones, headed by the Hocken Library of the University of Otago, Dunedin, such as the Auckland Institute and Museum; the Auckland Public Library; the Tauranga Public Library (Sladden collection); the Hawke's Bay Art Gallery and Museum (Russell Duncan collection); the Taranaki Museum; the Wanganui Regional Museum; the Canterbury Museum; the Canterbury Public Library; the Dunedin Public Library (McNab collection); the Hewitson Library, Knox College, Dunedin (Milligan collection); and the several university libraries. (Of interest to some may be reports on university libraries: W. J. McEldowney, *New Zealand University Library Resources: Report of a Survey carried out in 1972 for the New Zealand Vice-Chancellors' Committee*, Wellington, 1973, and its 1982 successor; while, perhaps even more interesting is A. D. Osborn, *New Zealand Library Resources*, Wellington, 1960, with its deplorable picture of the weaknesses of university libraries of the quite recent past.)

The **National Library** [www.natlib.govt.nz], with its vast collections of printed material, sound recordings, photographs, paintings and manuscripts, has the responsibility of collecting and preserving New Zealand's documentary heritage. It has, for example, the Dorothy Neal White collection of local and overseas children's books, and in its Music Room has videos, recordings and New Zealand's largest collection of orchestral parts and choral scores (— and cf. *A Guide to Music Reference Books for New Zealand Libraries*, by Roger Flury, Wellington, 1990; a selectively annotated guide to more than 200 works held in the Centre.) By law it receives — and lists in its *New Zealand National Bibliography* [see below **5.1.1**] — practically all items published in New Zealand: books, pamphlets, serials, newspapers, sheet music. It also lists recorded music in the *Bibliography*. The National Preservation Office, established by the Library in conjunction with the National Archives [below **9.3**], has been formed to maintain the country's heritage, its staff travelling the country and advising on the preservation of such material as newspapers, maps, books, photographs, along with sound recordings, video footage and digital information.

The National Library was established in 1966, combining three existing state libraries centred in Wellington: the National Library Service, the General Assembly (Parliamentary) Library and the Turnbull Library. But in subsequent years it has developed its own character and shed some of its original responsibilities. Education in librarianship, part of the original National Library Service from 1946, passed in 1980 to Victoria University of Wellington and the then Wellington Teachers College. The General Assembly/Parliamentary Library regained a separate, if now more focussed, identity in 1985. The National Library finally moved into permanent and purpose-built premises in 1987, the same year in which decision was made to end the Country Library Service, initially one of the major components of the old National Library Service, which since 1938 had bulk lent books to rural libraries. An offshoot, the school library service 1941–, subsequently was cut back. But the National Library continued to see as its responsibility assisting and supporting libraries through the country — through interloaning, computer online services, and access to its databases. [See too **Finding Maori Information: 10.2.3.**]

It was the collecting zeal of the merchant, Alexander Horsburgh **Turnbull** (1868-1918), and Dr. Thomas Morland **Hocken** (1836-1910) which provided the nucleus of New Zealand's two outstanding research libraries with their extensive holdings of private papers, maps and pictures as well as of early publications — newspapers, books, pamphlets, and so on. A helpful indication of the original character of these libraries is given in E. H. McCormick's 1960 Hocken Lecture, *The Fascinating Folly: Dr Hocken and his Fellow Collectors*, Dunedin, 1961, and in his biography, *Alexander Turnbull: His Life, his Circle, his Collections*, Wellington, 1974. W. H. Trimble's *Catalogue of the Hocken Library*, Dunedin, 1912, although outdated, remains a valuable outline of what still represents much of the most important material in that library; it was compiled in happy ignorance of modern cataloguing systems, and most of the collection now has been reclassified. There is no comparable catalogue for the Turnbull Library. Notes of accessions are included in the *Turnbull Library Record*, Wellington, 1940-1962, 1967–, and the card catalogues up to 1984 are available on microfiche [on which see **5.1.1**]. As a part of the National Library, the Alexander Turnbull Library continued and developed its role and scope, adding archives of music, cartoons, and oral history recordings to the library's original interests — which range beyond New Zealand and the Pacific to include what has been called 'the high culture of the Old World', most notably a John Milton collection of international standing. Among the Turnbull's considerable resources also are its Archive of New Zealand Music, with music manuscripts and heritage recordings, the Oral History Centre [below, **3.2**: Oral records], New Zealand Cartoon Archive. The Cartoon Archive, set up in 1992 with corporate sponsorship, produces its own *Quiplash*. A history of the Turnbull Library, including details about Alexander Turnbull himself and subsequent major donors to the library, is Rachel Barrowman's *The Turnbull: A Library and Its World*, Auckland, 1995.[See too **Finding Maori Information**: **10.2.2.**]

In *The Fascinating Folly*, McCormick also describes the collection of Sir George Grey, a third great collector and public benefactor, now housed within the Auckland Public Library. For further descriptions see Wynn Colgan, *The Governor's Gift: The Auckland Public Library 1880-1980*, Auckland, 1980, and Jack Bennett, 'The Grey collection', *New Zealand Libraries* 16 (1953): 82-6. [See too **10.2.4.**] There are brief studies of other important book collectors in *Book & Print in New Zealand: A Guide to Print Culture in Aotearoa New Zealand*, edited by Penny Griffith, Ross Harvey and Keith Maslen, Wellington, 1997 [noted, also **4.9**].

The Parliamentary Library holds the fullest range in New Zealand of local and overseas governmental and parliamentary material. From 1903 it has been a library of 'legal deposit', receiving copies of practically all New Zealand publications, although since 1987 the deposit office has been in the National Library. Previously, after its divorce in 1985 from the National Library, parliament's library had shed its unpublished private papers, numbers of old newspapers and many of its periodicals to the Turnbull and been placed under a newly established Parliamentary Service Commission, a committee of

MPs chaired by parliament's Speaker which is responsible for MPs' administrative and support services. With the 1986 change of the formal name of the legislature from 'General Assembly' to 'Parliament', the library similarly was renamed. The Parliamentary Library serves mainly MPs and parliamentary staff. Others wishing to use it should request permission in advance; usually one day's notice is sufficient.

A brief centennial account of the Library, 1858-1958, is included in the General Assembly Library's 1958 annual report (*Appendices to the Journals of the House of Representatives*, H. 32). In the nineteenth century the Library published a series of printed catalogues. The last one, the two-volume *Catalogue of the General Assembly Library of New Zealand*, Wellington, 1897 (together with a *Supplement*, 1899), remains the best guide to its nineteenth-century holdings.

Interlibrary loan

Thanks to interlibrary loan (or 'interloan' as it is commonly called) a researcher has access to almost all the books, periodicals, and theses held by any New Zealand library. One of the purposes, in fact, of bibliographic databases — that is, those that provide references to the literature, not full text — is to facilitate library interloan, and the same purpose also is served by a wide range of printed 'union lists' and 'union catalogues'. If need be, books, articles and theses, or microfilm or photo copies of them, can be obtained from libraries and document suppliers overseas (by mail, fax or electronically). Journal articles published since 1990, for example, may be obtained within a couple of days, although this may be costly. Libraries vary in the quality of service they provide, and older items may take quite a time in coming.

3.2 Directories and library holdings

A ranging discussion of New Zealand libraries by Brian McKeon, including development, governance, librarianship and much beside, is in P. Griffith et al. ed., *Book & Print in New Zealand*, [below **4.9**]. Libraries and information centres are listed in *DILSINZ: Directory of Information and Library Services in New Zealand*, by Paul Szentirmay and Thiam Ch'ng Szentirmay, 6th ed., Wellington, 1988. This is alphabetically ordered with several indexes. Among its valuable features is an index of libraries according to locality, showing for example the 28 centres in Christchurch alone. Unfortunately the late 1980s restructuring of local and central government has rendered some of the information out of date. From 1980, every two or three years the New Zealand Library Association, later the New Zealand Library and Information Association, produced *Public Libraries of New Zealand*, arranged by size of population served. The latest annual edition of the booklet *New Zealand Library Symbols*, issued by the National Library, can also serve as a library directory. From 1998 the Association became the Library and Information Association New Zealand Aotearoa (LIANZ).

R. B. Downs, *Australian and New Zealand Library Resources*, London and Melbourne, 1979, was the work of a visiting American librarian who relied heavily on published accounts and descriptions of library collections; as a result, its coverage is somewhat patchy and unbalanced. A useful feature is that it describes where different types of material may be found (as opposed to describing resources, library by library).

Archives and manuscripts

For **archives and manuscripts**, the best guide to the character of an institution's holdings — apart from any leaflet, brochure or other material produced by a library itself — is Frank Rogers, *Archives New Zealand: 4, A Directory of Archives and Manuscript Repositories in New Zealand, the Cook Islands, Fiji, Niue, Tokelau, Tonga and Western Samoa*, Plimmerton, 1992. This is a revised edition of a work first published in 1985, arranged geographically and intended to complement the *National Register of Archives and Manuscript Repositories in New Zealand* [below **Archives and manuscripts: 9.1**]. There were two supplementary volumes to the first edition (hence this is numbered 'Four'). The two were a 1985 report on statistics, and *Archives New Zealand: 3, Medicine and Public Health*, Plimmerton, 1990, a listing of archives repositories with descriptions of holdings likely to be of interest for the study of medicine and public health. Some of the descriptions in *Archives 3* — unlike in the first volume — are very full; see, for example, pp. 19-28 for the National Archives and pp. 30-40 for the Turnbull Library.

The Peace Movement Aotearoa has published a *Bibliography of Peace Archives*, compiled by Charlotte Fitzgerald and Peter Bowmar, Wellington, 1991 (which also includes a chronology of peace events and groups).

Maps

A comprehensive guide to New Zealand **map collections** is Brian Marshall, *Map Making and Map Keeping in New Zealand: a review and bibliography*, Auckland, 1992.

Music

The principal **music** collections — notably the Archive of New Zealand Music in the Turnbull Library — publish progress reports and lists of acquisitions from time to time in *Crescendo*, 1982–, the bulletin of the New Zealand branch of the International Association of Music Libraries. [See too on the Audio Visual Arts and Science Museum, below **9.5**.]

Oral records

[note also **9.5**: Broadcasting]

Over the past fifteen to twenty years **oral history** has become a major growth area in New Zealand research collections. Increased interest in social history, particularly in the history of those who were not well represented in the documentary sources traditionally used by historians, led to the seeking out and recording of a variety of oral recollections. On the air, and in print, past recordings have been re-presented.

Many research bodies are building up their oral archives; the most extensive collection of oral history recordings in New Zealand, however, is in the Turnbull Library which by the 1990s had over 3,000 hours of spoken recordings on discs, reels and cassette tape. Included in this collection are the recordings of the former New Zealand Oral History Archive, a series of interviews with New Zealand composers and musicians, recordings of radio programmes such as 'Open Country' and 'Spectrum', and many recordings created by private donors. This collection is also the official repository for all recordings created by recipients of grants from the Australian Sesquicentennial gift administered by the Historical Branch of the Department of Internal Affairs. Access is provided by a database containing very extensive detail about the collection and allowing full text searches, and accessions are noted in the *Turnbull Library Record.*

Pioneers in developing oral history records were Hugo Manson, Judith Fyfe and Jean Harton who set up the first oral history archives in the early 1980s. For a decade they worked to build up their organisation, recording ordinary people in their every day lives — people who normally in the past would not get on record. Subsequently the New Zealand Oral History Archive trust board was disestablished and the archives became part of the Oral History Centre at the Turnbull Library. Besides acting as a repository for this large oral history collection, the Turnbull Library has taken over the activities of the Oral History Archive. It undertakes an annual recording programme, records and processes oral histories for commercial clients, and is active in raising standards — technological and methodological — and advising on ethics, through its educational and advisory services. In the 1990s the Centre has received an avalanche of material for all around the country. As well as recording life, community and organisations' histories, the Oral History Centre is involved in recording contemporary history, talking to a number of well-known New Zealanders about their current activities. In some cases interviewees impose access restrictions — perhaps up to 50 years in the case of political recordings, but the overwhelming bulk of the material is open to the public.

Since 1986 the National Oral History Association (NOHANZ, Box 3819, Postal Centre, Wellington) has been active. The Association has published a Code of Ethical Practice and has kept oral historians up to date with work here and overseas through its newsletters and conferences. The National Oral History Association in conjunction with the Turnbull Library has reported in the National Oral History Association of New Zealand's *Oral History in New Zealand: a directory of collections 1992*, Wellington, 1992, results of a survey seeking to identify and report oral history recordings held in institutional and private collections throughout the country.

On the management of oral history collections, see especially Alan Ward, *A Manual of Sound Archive Administration*, Aldershot, 1990; *Managing Archives and Archival Institutions*, ed. James Gregory Bradsher, London, 1988; and Frederick Stielow, *The Management of Oral History Sound Archives*, Westport, Connecticut, 1986.

Pictures and photographs

The most extensive holdings of **pictorial material** — if very largely not put out in public display — are in the Turnbull and Hocken Libraries. Samples have been reproduced as prints — over the years the Turnbull's Endowment Trust published series taken from its paintings and photographs. The Hocken Library has over 12,000 works of art relating to New Zealand and the Pacific dating from the eighteenth century to the present day, and over 1,000,000 photographs from the mid nineteenth century, including the work of modern photo-artists. The Turnbull's some 60,000 paintings, drawings and prints relating to New Zealand and the Pacific are available on the computerised database Tapuhi. Major acquisitions have been noted in the *Turnbull Library Record* since 1969. On artists' biographies, the Turnbull Library has an index to published and unpublished information, and the Hector Library at Te Papa (of which the former National Art Gallery Resource Centre is now part) has newspaper clippings and other information on artists and art history. The Turnbull also holds architectural plans and art ephemera, and it has a collection of some 20,000 photographs of eighteenth and nineteenth-century paintings, drawings and prints relating to New Zealand. The originals are held by the Turnbull, other New Zealand collections, private collectors, and overseas institutions such as the Mitchell Library and the British Library: this was described in *ARLIS/ANZ News*, June 1983, a publication of the Arts Libraries Societies, Australia and New Zealand.

The Turnbull Library has a colour transparency service for art-works held in Drawings and Prints, and can supply black-and-white and colour prints of works held in both the photograph and the art collections (and on computer imaging see above [2.2]). Other institutions such as the Hocken Library and the Auckland City Art Gallery provide similar services.

There is an out-of-date *Catalogue of Pictures in the Hocken Library*, compiled by Jean McGill and Linda Rodda, Dunedin, 1948, and a typed *Catalogue of the Picture Collection,* 1970, published by the Auckland Institute and Museum. In addition to the Hocken and Turnbull Libraries, Te Papa, the national museum, has an extensive photograph collection, and there are splendid collections in some regional museums, for example the Nelson Museum (in particular the Tyree collection) and the Auckland Institute and Museum. Private businesses, local authorities and central government departments also have accumulated impressive numbers of photographs, which are now deposited in their archives or in the National Archives, to which also have passed large photograph collections from the former government departments, Railways and the Forest Service, and some of the collection of the National Publicity Studios (now privatised and sold to DAC Group Ltd.) The results of a questionnaire sent to 350 institutions is a revised *Directory of New Zealand Photograph Collections*, compiled by the pictorial reference service of the Alexander Turnbull Library, Wellington, 1992.

[On film see below **4.9** Culture reference works, and **9.5**.]

3.3 Library classification and cataloguing

The two major international subject classification schemes by which library items are classified are of comparatively recent origin. The first edition of the Dewey Decimal Classification was published by Melvil Dewey in 1876. This scheme is widely used in New Zealand public libraries, in the National Library, and in the libraries of Auckland and Massey universities. The other important system in use is that developed by the Library of Congress, which is used in the other university libraries. There are some other general classification schemes in use in New Zealand, most notably the Universal Decimal Classification which is used mainly in special libraries.

In searching a library catalogue, a rudimentary knowledge of library cataloguing rules can be helpful. Today, libraries follow standard rules laid down in the 670-page revised second edition of the *Anglo-American Cataloguing Rules* (1988 — new revision pending). These rules are used extensively in the English-speaking world.

A catalogue record will look something like that shown here:

ITEM NUMBER	221404
AUTHOR	Sinclair, Keith, 1922-1993.
TITLE	A history of New Zealand / Keith Sinclair.
EDITION	4th rev. ed.
PUBLISHER	Auckland, N.Z. : Penguin Books, 1991.
PHYS DESC	364 p. : maps ; 20 cm.

NOTES On cover: New edition.
  Includes index.
  Includes bibliographical references (p. [346]-351).

SUBJECT(S)	1. New Zealand -- History.

DU/420/SL23/1991

An old-style card catalogue probably will be laid out in comparable fashion.

Cataloguers use as the basis for the entry for a person's name the form of the name most commonly used by that author on the title pages of his or her works. Additions such as extra forenames, title and date of birth are given if they can be readily ascertained. Sometimes some perseverance — and patience — is required to find a desired entry, perhaps by moving from author search to title, or from title to key words. A searcher for the autobiography of the former Labour M.P., G. H. O. Wilson, for example, probably will only find it under 'Wilson, Ormond', following the name under which he wrote. But the author of *Station Life in New Zealand* may well not be found under her pen name 'Lady Barker' [Barker, Lady], nor under her name 'Mary Anne Broome', but under 'Barker, Mary Anne'. (Mary Anne Stewart married George Barker, later Sir George; widowed, she later married Frederick Broome but nonetheless wrote as 'Lady Barker'.) The political scientist Keith Jackson may be catalogued as Jackson, W. K. (William Keith). The historian F. L. W. Wood may appear in one entry with his 'W' spelt Whitfeld and in another, as another person as it were, 'Whitfield'. This variation is a reminder of the ease with which reference works can acquire and retain a mistake — as Wood's name can be seen to change in later editions of *Who's Who*. Of course the researcher naturally assumes that the subject of a *Who's Who* entry will always check copy, and will never herself, or himself, carelessly give wrong information: and the researcher will be wrong on both counts.

Apart from details concerning the author, most of the rest of the information in a catalogue entry normally is taken from the book itself. The title is taken from the book's title page — not from the spine or the cover, or there could be confusion. A publication on 'crown lands' by a famous publishing house had on the dust-cover 'church' lands. W. P. Morrell's *The Provincial System in New Zealand, 1852-1876* in its first edition had on the cover *The Provincial System of Government* ... (Such a work normally will, of course, be entered under 'P' for 'Provincial', not 'T' for 'The', and Maori-language works similarly normally will not be entered under 'T' for 'Te' or 'N' for 'Nga'.)

From the catalogue record for the book by Keith Sinclair it can be seen that it is of good length (364 pages), the size of a typical paperback (20 cm high). It was written by a man of advanced years, but perhaps the earlier edition was written much earlier (as in fact it was — either way the age of the author may be indicative both of stature and of approach). It was published by a reputable publisher and the popular character of the work, specifically for a New Zealand audience, is shown by the number of editions it has been through. It is given one simple subject heading, 'New Zealand—History': apparent also to someone familiar with the Library of Congress system by the classification 'DU/420'. Frequent library users soon become familiar with the subject classifications which are likely to be of most use to them. (SL23 is the 'Cutter' number given to Keith Sinclair while 1991, of course, refers to the date of this edition.) Finally, the book has a five-page bibliography which would indicate a scholarly attitude on the part of the author. Finally, further information may be found on a second 'page' of the record.

Libraries may still have old material catalogued only on cards, or on microfiche. Progressively, however, most material is being converted to computer files, to Online Public Access Catalogues (OPAC). Though having to use a computer sometimes may be a mixed blessing, OPACs greatly assist with the finding of information, not least because it is now possible to search for book titles, series titles, subject-headings, and so on. Note, however, that a number of different OPAC systems are in use in New Zealand libraries; users may need to spend a little time ensuring that they can use a particular library's OPAC to best advantage.

The user of a library catalogue will find both frustration and helpful aids in the pursuit of awkward items. For example if the OPAC comes up with a great long list of items sometimes it can be instructed to sort them — by date of publication, or author, and so forth.

OPACs generally offer a keyword search option which helps finding corporate names: an important point is that organisations can be 'authors'. Other useful features of OPACs may be ability to call up 'related works', and ability to search works according to their classification: through the online catalogue the searcher can browse forwards or backward to see what other library items have the same or nearly the same classification given to them.

For older works searchers may have to show some ingenuity in tracking items down in old card catalogues, especially since over the years cataloguing rules have changed. Even today **official documents** can elude all but the most persistent. Mostly government publications are entered under the name of the territory governed (for example 'New Zealand'), and the various departments and ministries are given as subheadings (for example, 'New Zealand. Ministry of Foreign Affairs and Trade'. But government departments change their names, subdivide, merge: 'New Zealand. Ministry of External Relations' and 'Department of Trade and Industry' also will be headings in the catalogue; so may be 'New Zealand. Dept. ...', or simply 'Department of ...'). Where an official publication has a book-like title, such as *Tomorrow's Schools: the reform of education administration in New Zealand*, it may be found under that entry as well as buried in a long list of 'Dept.' (rather perhaps than 'Department' or, later, 'Ministry') 'of Education' publications. In the non-governmental world items may also be found under the names of corporate bodies (such as 'Polynesian Society'); conferences are regarded as corporate bodies if they have a name, and are catalogued under the name. Normally, however, they will be found under the appropriate organisation: 'Geological Society of New Zealand. Conference (1993: Victoria University of Wellington)'.

One item of information universally used but which may not be found in the catalogue is the ten-digit **ISBN** (international standard book number) allocated to a book. The ISBN is divided into four parts: the first part — of one to three digits — identifies the language or geographical area in which the book was published; the second — of two to seven digits, depending on the size of the publisher — identifies the publisher (in New Zealand allocated by the National Library); the third identifies the particular title and binding; and the fourth, the check digit, is used in a computer analysis to pick up errors in transcribing the other nine digits.

4. Reference Works

4.1 Guides and aids

The weighty American and British volumes, the American Library Association's

- *Guide to Reference Books*, 11th ed., edited by Robert Balay, Chicago, 1996

and the two-volume

- *Walford's Guide to Reference Material* of the Library Association in Great Britain ed., 7th ed., edited by Marilyn Mullay and Priscilla Schlicke, London, 1996

provide annotated lists of reference works such as bibliographies, indexes, library catalogues, dictionaries, encyclopedias, atlases, and so forth. (Earlier editions of *Walford's Guide* were, not surprisingly, edited by A. J. Walford.)

The nearest thing we have in New Zealand to these massive compilations is the

- *Guide to New Zealand Information Sources*, Palmerston North, 1975-82.

This multi-part work was organised by the Massey University Library and published in eight booklets, on: plants and animals; farming, field

and agricultural crops; livestock farming, fisheries, and forestry; education; religion; official publications (new edition 1994); history; and geography. The Massey series largely superseded the even more outdated John Harris's *Guide to New Zealand Reference Material and Other Sources of Information*, 2nd ed., Wellington, 1950, with its *Supplements* (1951 and 1956) by A. G. Bagnall. [Mentioned below **5.1.1** is J. E. Traue, *New Zealand Studies: A Guide to Bibliographic Resources.*]
Progressively researchers will be directed to electronic sources for their information. For example, in addition to such solid compilations as *Finding Social Science Research: an information directory*, compiled by Dallas and Vasantha Krishnan, Wellington, [1994], there is a growing number of slim directories like the loose-leaf *Environmental Directory: databases and collections*, published by Statistics New Zealand, Wellington, 1996– [**4.4**] (cf. **4.8** on business sources, and **4.11** on science, etc.).

4.2 Encyclopedias

Although there have been later publications, the most comprehensive and valuable New Zealand encyclopedia is still

• *An Encyclopaedia of New Zealand*, ed. A. H. McLintock, 3 vols, Wellington, 1966.

This contains signed articles — of varying quality — with brief bibliographies, and has a comprehensive index. No reference work, however impressively factual, is infallible, and just as it is salutary to read Harvey Einbinder's critique of the *Encyclopaedia Britannica* (*The Myth of the Britannica*, London, 1964), so the article on McLintock's encyclopaedia by J. W. Winchester in the journal *Comment*, December, 1968, is worth reading. Inescapably, too, we 'betray ourselves more clearly in works of reference than in other literary productions.... the Encyclopedia Britannica, established in 1768 as the British Empire got under way, displays what are now thought to be classic "orientalists" perspectives: crudely put, it takes a one-sided view of other cultures while hoping to be panoptic'.[1]
No revised edition of the *Encyclopaedia of New Zealand* has been published or is planned. The *Bateman New Zealand Encyclopedia*, edited by Gordon McLauchlan, 4th ed., Auckland, 1995, and its stable-mate, *The Illustrated Encyclopedia of New Zealand*, ed. Gordon McLauchlan, Auckland, 1992, are both single-volume works aimed towards a popular readership, and available on CD-ROM. Older now but still useful in pursuit of a range of topics is what might be described as an encyclopedia of New Zealand history:

---

1 Giles Foden, in *Guardian Weekly*, March 22, 1998, p. 32.

• *New Zealand's Heritage: The Making of a Nation*, ed. R. Knox, Wellington, 1971-73, reprinted with minor amendments, 1977-1979.

Both *The Illustrated Encyclopedia* and *New Zealand's Heritage* were originally published as part-works, the latter appearing in 105 parts as a handsome weekly magazine, sold through corner dairies and the like. For scholarly purposes, *New Zealand's Heritage* is, of the two, not only the more accessible (through an index, separately published) but the more substantial and trustworthy.

A legal encyclopedia, more useful than its name might imply, is *Butterworths N. Z. Law Dictionary*, 4th ed., ed. Peter Spiller. (Derived from the English *Concise Law Dictionary*, 1876–, the New Zealand version first appeared as *Mozley and Whiteley's Law Dictionary: New Zealand Edition*, ed. G. W. Hinde, Wellington, 1964, changing in the following editions — 2nd, 1972; 3rd, 1979;'revised 3rd.', 1986 — to *New Zealand Law Dictionary*). (*New Zealand Law Who's Who* is a directory of lawyers and law firms.) The ancient *Cyclopedia of New Zealand: Industrial, Descriptive, Historical, Biographical, Facts, Figures, Illustrations*, 6 vols, Wellington and Christchurch, 1897-1908, is a compendium of information, gathered together at the turn of the century, and organised by provinces. A Southern — Otago and Southland — repetition with, as previously, entries sold to would-be entrants, is appearing for the 150th anniversary of the Otago settlement.

Margaret Orbell has produced *The Illustrated Encyclopedia of Maori Myth and Legend*, 1995, and there are other specialist encyclopedias — for example, *The Encyclopedia of New Zealand Rugby* compiled by Rod Chester, Ron Palenski and Neville McMillan, 2nd. ed., Auckland, 1987.

4.3 Dictionaries

Dictionaries track the evolution of language, and with it cultural changes, showing the forces that have shaped the society and, in the case of recent editions, pointing to modern concepts and preoccupations. Moreover, dictionaries are not neutral records of language. As an English writer has pointed out, odd as it may seem to describe a dictionary as political, or as telling a story, in fact almost all of them have been. Mostly 'their history has been about national self-consciousness'[1] — although there are some produced more for entertainment or amusement, such as David McGill's *Complete Kiwi Slang Dictionary*, Auckland, 1998.

---

1   Andrew Marr, *Observer*, 16 August 1998.

Today standard dictionaries, including multi-language dictionaries, are readily accessible on the Internet. But for the researcher these do not supersede specialist and older printed works, and the story they tell.

The first significant Australasian dictionary was E. E. Morris's *Austral-English: A Dictionary of Australasian Words, Phrases and Usages* ('with those aboriginal Australian and Maori words which have become incorporated in the language ...'), London, 1898. A later well-known work is S. J. Baker's *New Zealand Slang: A Dictionary of Colloquialisms*, Christchurch, 1941. Quite fun to browse through is *The New Zealand Dictionary*, edited by Elizabeth and Harry Orsman, Auckland 1994, which lists only words and phrases which 'are in some way distinctively ... part of the spoken or written language of English-speaking New Zealanders'. Three years on, there followed the substantial

- *The Dictionary of New Zealand English: A Dictionary of New Zealandisms on Historical Principles*, ed H. W. Orsman. Auckland, 1997

a work, forty years in the making which, in the modest words of its publisher, 'is an essential reference and educational resource for all those interested in New Zealand society, history and culture'. New Zealandisms are words originating in New Zealand, having a special New Zealand meaning or having a special significance for New Zealand history. Entries and quotations are arranged chronologically. Following launch of the new dictionary, Victoria University and Oxford University Press announced as a joint venture setting up of the New Zealand Dictionary Centre. The Centre's role is to update the dictionary database, conduct research, and publish dictionaries and related educational materials. It also produces its newsletter, *NZWords*. The New Zealand Centre follows previous establishment of an Australian Dictionary Centre [below **4.13**].

Of older and smaller dictionaries of New Zealand English, the *Heinemann New Zealand Dictionary*, ed. H. W. Orsman, Auckland, 1979, 2nd ed. 1989, led the field, but several other one-volume dictionaries were published in the 1980s: *Collins New Zealand Compact Dictionary of the English Language*, ed. Ian A. Gordon, Auckland, 1985; *Penguin Tasman Dictionary and International Dictionary for all New Zealanders*, general ed. A. Delbridge, New Zealand consulting ed. H. W. Orsman, Auckland, 1986; *The New Zealand Pocket Oxford Dictionary*, ed. Robert Burchfield, 1986, reprinted with corrections, Auckland, 1990. This last, in its fat second edition, ed. Tony Deverson, Auckland, 1997, is based on the *Australian Oxford Pocket Dictionary* and the *Pocket Oxford English Dictionary* and draws upon Orsman's *Dictionary of New Zealand English*. Tony Deverson has also edited *The New Zealand Oxford*

Paperback Dictionary, 1998. Note, too, for legal terminology, the *Butterworths New Zealand Law Dictionary* along with the British *Concise Law Dictionary* [above, **4.2**].

Until superseded by the Orsman *Dictionary*, a rich source of examples of New Zealand words and usage was in the *Supplement*, ed. R. W. Burchfield, 4 vols, 1972-86, of the *Oxford English Dictionary*. The *Oxford English Dictionary* is, of course, a basic and essential dictionary for New Zealand as well as for British scholars. An integrated second edition, prepared by J. A. Simpson and E. S. C. Weiner, in which the supplements are merged with the main alphabetical sequence, was published in 20 volumes in 1989 and sold at a four-figure price, and is also available on CD-ROM, or in a cheaper 'compact' edition to be read with a magnifying glass.

For the student of Maori, well-known works are H. W. Williams, *A Dictionary of the Maori Language*, 7th rev. ed., Wellington, 1971 (with later reprints); Bruce Biggs, *The Complete English-Maori Dictionary*, Auckland, 1981, reprinted with corrections 1985 and later; P. M. Ryan, *The Dictionary of Modern Maori*, 2nd ed., Auckland, 1997; H. M. Ngata, *English-Maori Dictionary*, Wellington, 1993. The Maori Language Commission, whose tasks include developing new terms in Maori as required, has published its dictionary of contemporary Maori words: *Te Matatiki*, Auckland, 1996.

[See also below **4.13**: Australian and British reference material.]

4.4 Chronologies

Chronologies are included in the *New Zealand Official Yearbook* [below **4.10**], fullest references being given to the most recent events; material from later editions can be supplemented from earlier editions. There is also a New Zealand volume in the *Historical Dictionary* series published by Scarecrow Press: *Historical Dictionary of New Zealand*, by Keith Jackson and Alan McRobie, Auckland 1996. For political and official dates note also *New Zealand Parliamentary Record* and *Ministers and Members in the New Zealand Parliament* [**4.10**]. Together with these other reference works, the *Yearbook* may be used to find most of the major and many of the minor dates in New Zealand history — and normally these authorities can be relied upon to be accurate. There is a series of chronologies, 1840–, in the 'Politics and the State' section of David C. Thorns and Charles P. Sedgwick, *Understanding Aotearoa/New Zealand: Historical Statistics*, Palmerston North, 1997 [**4.12**].

A substantial chronological compilation is *The New Zealand Book of Events*, devised and edited by Bryce Fraser, Auckland, 1986, which comprises a series of chronologies, divided into 14 sections. More selective is *Two Hundred Years of New Zealand History, 1769-*

1969: Sampler Chronology, compiled by A. W. Reed, Wellington, 1979. A twenty-two page 'Chronology' is included in W. B. Sutch's *Poverty and Progress in New Zealand: A Reassessment*, 2nd rev. ed., Wellington, 1969, and two older strictly chronological works are Allan Sutherland's *New Zealand Famous Firsts and Related Records*, Wellington, 1960, and George Finn's *Datus: A Chronology of New Zealand from the Time of the Moa*, Auckland, 1931 (although a work which dates events of pre-recorded history must necessarily rely upon legends — of which there are many). There is a *Chronology: New Zealand in the War, 1939-1946*, compiled by Robin Kay, Wellington, 1968. *The New Zealand Book of Records*, compiled by Jonathan Eisen and Katherine Joyce Smith, Auckland, 1994, is catalogued by librarians 'Subjects: Curiosities and wonders'. A comprehensive chronological survey of concrete use in New Zealand is Geoffrey Thornton, *Cast in Concrete*, 1997 [below **4.5**].

For half a century, until the 1960s, the *Round Table*, London, 1910–, published quarterly surveys of events in New Zealand and the other 'dominions' (to use an outdated terminology); there is an index for the years 1910-35. To a degree the later gap was filled by the *Reserve Bank of New Zealand Bulletin* [www.rbnz.govt.nz] (initially *Reserve Bank Bulletin*), Wellington, 1938–, which had published economic surveys, at quarterly or six-monthly intervals, since 1952. From 1998 statistical tables were published separately in the Bank's new quarterly *Financial Statistics*. (The Bank also produces a *Weekly Statistical Release*, 1981–.) Discussions of the state of the New Zealand economy will also be found in the publications of the New Zealand Institute of Economic Research as well as in papers produced by banks and economic forecasters.

For industrial relations there is a Chronicle published in the *New Zealand Journal of Industrial Relations*, 1976–. A little publication designed to inform expatriates is the monthly *Newzgram*, Christchurch, 1993–. There are also brief New Zealand summaries — on parliamentary affairs — in the journal *Parliamentarian*, and note also *The Table*, 1932–, the publication of the clerks of Commonwealth parliaments. Unrivalled as a factual record of events over a world range is *Keesing's Record of World Events* (formerly *Keesing's Contemporary Archives*, but retitled and redesigned in 1989), London, 1931–: well-indexed, and well signposted with 'previous' references. As well as the frequent print updates, it is available on CD-ROM with quarterly updating. Reuters is offered online by some libraries, and has a decade-long backfile. Also useful for setting an international context for New Zealand events is the renowned British *The Annual Register*, London, 1758–. Note, too, encyclopedia year-books [mentioned below: **4.13**].

4.5 Atlases, gazetteers, maps and guides

At last, in the late 1990s, there has appeared a work which began as a 1940 centennial project: an historical atlas of New Zealand, for long deferred as one of the victims of war and post-war economies. Produced in the Historical Branch of the Department of Internal Affairs, the

- *Bateman New Zealand Historical Atlas: Ko Papatuanuku e Takoto Nei*, edited by Malcolm McKinnon with Barry Bradley and Russell Kirkpatrick, Auckland, 1997

is a large, 283-page, coffee-table style work. Following its publication, New Zealand studies can never be the same: it is a brilliant effort. Colour maps, graphs, charts, diagrams, with accompanying text, are packed with eye-breaking information. To illuminate, or perhaps to jolt the viewer, many maps are presented in unconventional format, such as 'upside down'. The atlas, says its editor, 'is intended to work at many different levels of explanation — international, national, regional, local'. Particular regional experiences are picked out in some cases, while in others a locality or region is chosen for its representative character. The work is divided into five periods: pre-human, 'Te Ao Maori', 'Colony and Colonised', 'Dominion', and modern ('From Progress to Uncertainty').

Of other, more conventional atlases, the best is the *Heinemann New Zealand Atlas*, ed. D. McKenzie, Auckland, 1987. The descriptive *New Zealand Atlas*, ed. Ian Wards, Wellington, 1976, replaces but does not entirely supersede the older *A Descriptive Atlas of New Zealand*, ed. A. H. McLintock, Wellington, 1959.

For all the impressive range of information in the *New Zealand Historical Atlas*, use may still be found for older and more specialised works. For example, a fascinating little book is John Yonge, *New Zealand Railway and Tramway Atlas*, 4th ed., Exeter, 1993. An excellent guide to land use information (maps, valuation, statistics) is the *Land Information Handbook*, Wellington, Land Use Advisory Council, 1977.

On electorate boundaries, see Alan McRobie, *New Zealand Electoral Atlas*, Wellington, 1989. Handy, and quite intriguing, are the 42 different maps of New Zealand in the booklet issued by the Local Government Commission, *Regions and Districts of New Zealand. Areas adopted to date for various administrative and research purposes,* [Wellington], 1973. For a slightly earlier guide to boundaries relevant for official statistics — and main types of data published for each — there is the *Atlas of New Zealand Regional Statistics*, published by the Town and Country Planning Branch of the Ministry of Works (Wellington, 1968). The later loose-leaf *Atlas of*

New Zealand Boundaries with text by Brian Marshall and maps by Jan Kelly, Auckland, 1986–, showed the variety of ways New Zealand was divided up for administrative purposes. It was updated irregularly, and had an historical series of local government boundaries and eventually was replaced by the hardback, 325-page new

- *Atlas of New Zealand Boundaries* by Jan Kelly and Brian Marshall, Auckland, 1996

whose comprehensive coverage ranges through such diverse topics as the Environment (with for example High Seas Forecast Areas), Transport (including Ansett New Zealand Sales Areas), Finance (ANZ Bank Zones and Districts) to Religion, Learning and Sport (Netball New Zealand Regions)

For maps of New Zealand's neighbours there is the handsome *Atlas of the South Pacific*, 2nd ed., Wellington, 1986.

The official body responsible for determining, and changing, place names is the New Zealand Geographic Board, now part of Land Information New Zealand. The Board has a database, which can be consulted, and publishes name changes in the *New Zealand Gazette* [cited below **7.1.1**]. On microfiche, first published in book form, in 1968, is the *Gazetteer of N. Z. Place Names*, Wellington, 1990–, giving place names as shown on official maps published by the Department of Lands and Survey, later Department of Survey and Land Information and now Land Information New Zealand. The software package Terraview contains data sourced from Land Information New Zealand, identifying the location, dimensions and ownership of properties, and their valuations — of obvious use to the New Zealand Fire Service in particular.

Discover New Zealand: a Wises Guide, 9th ed., Auckland, 1994 (previously *Wises New Zealand Guide: A Gazetteer of New Zealand*, and in earlier editions — 1952, 1957, 1962 — E. S. Dollimore, *The New Zealand Guide*), gives a comprehensive list of places in New Zealand, with description and location, and the possible meanings of Maori place names. A. W. Reed produced a solid *Place Names of New Zealand*, Wellington, 1975, with a *Supplement*, Wellington, 1979 and, now updated, *The Reed Dictionary of Maori Place Names*, *Te papakupu ingoa wahi Maori a Reed*, 3rd ed., Auckland, 1996. In *He Korero Purakau mo nga Taunahanahatanga a nga Tupuna/Place Names of the Ancestors: a Maori Oral History Atlas*, Wellington, 1990, Maori place names are elucidated in the light of Maori tradition, with maps, illustrations, and text in Maori and English. Published in conjunction with this atlas is a simpler booklet, *Nga Tohu Pumahara/The Survey Pegs of the Past: Understanding Maori Place Names*, compiled by Te Aue Davis, Tipene O'Regan and John Wilson, Wellington, 1990.

To track down former place names, useful are such older works as the predecessor to the modern *Wises Guide 'Discover New Zealand'*: the *Wise's Index to Every Place in New Zealand*, Dunedin, 1899–, although to find places which were re-christened before last century, it may be necessary to refer to early maps. There are some guides to historical maps, such as *Maps of Canterbury and the West Coast: A Selected Bibliography*, produced by the map bibliography committee of the Canterbury branch, New Zealand Geographical Society, Christchurch, 1958. (Note also *Maps in the Canterbury Museum Library: A Subject Catalogue*, compiled by Brian Lovell-Smith, Christchurch, 1982.) The Otago branch of the New Zealand Geographical Society has produced *The Mapping of Otago*, Dunedin, 1947, and there are various compilations by the Otago geographer R. P. Hargreaves:

> *French Explorers' Maps of New Zealand*, London, 1966
> *Historical Maps of New Zealand; A Guide to the Map Exhibition held in the Otago Museum ... August 1964*, Dunedin, 1964
> *Maps in the Appendices to the Journals, House of Representatives: A Chronological Listing*, Dunedin, 1968 [see **10.5.2**]
> *Maps of New Zealand Appearing in British Parliamentary Papers*, Dunedin, 1962
> *Maps in New Zealand Provincial Council Papers*, Dunedin, 1964
> *Nineteenth Century French Hydrographic Charts of New Zealand*, Dunedin, 1966
> *Nineteenth Century British Hydrographic Charts of New Zealand*, Dunedin, 1969
> *Nineteenth Century Otago and Southland Town Plans*, Dunedin, 1968, and *Supplement*, Dunedin, 1971

There are also hydrographic appendices in J. O'C. Ross, *This Stern Coast: The Story of the Charting of the New Zealand Coast*, Wellington, 1969.

A comprehensive reference work, already cited [**3.2**], is

• Brian Marshall, *Map Making and Map Keeping in New Zealand: a review and bibliography*, Auckland, 1992.

It really is necessary, however, to refer to library staff for guidance on a library's holdings of maps. The Turnbull Library, the Hocken Library and the National Archives all have extensive map collections. Along with the successor to the Department of Survey and Land Information, Land Information New Zealand, National Archives holds the official central government map collections. Land Information New Zealand, LINZ, was formed in June 1996, as an amalgamation of the Department of Survey and Land Information with the Land Titles Office of the Department of Justice; commercial activities went to the new enterprise Terralink. LINZ retains some archives of the old Survey and Land Information Department. There is an inventory of these and a database is being compiled. There are computerised indexes to the Crown Purchase Deeds, Maori Land

Court titles, and other miscellaneous plans. These can be used free by on-site researchers, in Wellington — others have to pay.

Since 1968 the New Zealand Oceanographic Institute has published a *List of Charts* (originally *List of Available Charts*), today as part of the NIWA (National Institute of Water and Atmospheric Research) [cf. below **4.11**: Science] series.

There are numerous attractive illustrated guides to New Zealand's past, of which notable examples are the 'coffee table' publications of the Historic Places Trust: *The A. A. Book of New Zealand Historic Places*, Auckland, 1984, and the two-volume *Historic Buildings of New Zealand: North Island*, and *South Island*, Auckland, 1983. Less ambitious is the 80-page *Historic New Zealand*, Christchurch 1980, reprinted Auckland 1981, 1985, with photography by Warren Jacobs, Lloyd Park and Robin Smith and text by Errol Brathwaite. The Historic Places Trust also produces a series of booklets, such as the 32-page booklets on *Historic Wellington: a walking tour*, by Gavin McLean, *Historic Christchurch: a walking tour*, by John Wilson, and *Historic Bay of Islands: a driving tour*, by Fergus Clunie (all published 1998).

For walking about and exploring at ground level — or driving past historic localities — the best guides are the excellent D. and J. Pope, *Mobil New Zealand Travel Guide: North Island*, 9th ed., Auckland, 1996, and *Mobil New Zealand Travel Guide: South Island, Stewart Island and the Chatham Islands*, 7th ed., Auckland, 1995. Since 1977, too, there has been a fat *New Zealand* volume in the *lonely planet travel survival kit,* which like the Mobil guides is regularly updated. Lonely Planet also, since 1982, has produced a New Zealand walking guide, *Tramping in New Zealand.* Another well-known travel series, now also including a fat New Zealand volume, is Rough Guides, with *New Zealand: the Rough Guide*, compiled by Laura Harper, Tony Mudd and Paul Whitfield, 1998. Updates can be found on the Internet [www.roughguides.com].

Specific in focus are works by Geoffrey Thornton, *New Zealand's Industrial Heritage*, 1982, *The New Zealand Heritage of Farm Buildings,* 1986, and *Cast in Concrete: Concrete construction in New Zealand 1850-1939,* 1997.

4.6 Almanacs and street directories

An excellent reference work was the short-lived *Air New Zealand Almanac*, Auckland, 1982-89. Although now very out of date, it still has useful information not assembled elsewhere, for example in the sections on arts and on sport (— although for cricket there is the specialist superb annual *New Zealand Cricket Almanack*). The *Air New Zealand Almanac* followed on what once had been a major genre of publication. No student of the nineteenth century, for example, once introduced to the Hocken Library's large holdings of almanacs, could fail to appreciate these handbooks with their wealth of miscellaneous information: the listing of almanacs and directories in W. H. Trimble's *Catalogue of the Hocken Library* remains a valuable guide to their range. For a full guide there is A. G. Bagnall ed., *New Zealand National Bibliography to the year 1960* [see **5.1.1**].

There are also district and street directories: since the last decades of the nineteenth century there have been published regional directories containing alphabetical lists of residents, by district, and street directories, notably *Wise's New Zealand Post Office Directory*, Dunedin, 1872/3– and the now defunct *Stone's* directories. The *Union List of Serials* is the best guide to library holdings of almanacs and directories.

There is a section on directories in P. Griffith et al. ed., *Book & Print in New Zealand,* [below **4.9**]. And available from the author (12 Poplar Grove, Thorndon, Wellington, 6001) is *The Directory Directory: The Family, Local and Social Historian's Guide to Contents and Holdings of New Zealand Almanac, Business, Postal and Telephone Directories, 1842-1960*, Wellington, 1997, a 107-page historical account.

4.7 Biography and genealogy

The New Zealand centennial in 1940 (centennial, that is, of British annexation) was celebrated — even if celebration was somewhat subdued by the 1939-45 war — with both festivity and state-sponsored learned publications. G. H. Scholefield ed., *A Dictionary of New Zealand Biography*, 2 vols, Wellington, 1940, appeared as an official centennial publication; fifty years later, for the sesquicentenary in 1990, a comprehensive multi-volume dictionary of biography was organised. In 1983 a small unit was set up in Wellington in the Department of Internal Affairs. Professor W. H. Oliver was appointed first editor, subsequently succeeded by Dr Claudia Orange. Much of the work was carried out by voluntary committees set up through the country, and by a host of researchers and writers. The selection policy adopted for

• *The Dictionary of New Zealand Biography*, Wellington, 1990–

is somewhat broader than that found in comparable overseas (British, Australian and Canadian) publications. As well as providing biographies of well-known people, the *Dictionary* is also intended to give an insight into the scope of New Zealand society, not merely an introduction to its élites. Reader aids include a categories index, a tribal and hapu index and a nominal index. For the categories index, which is restricted to the subjects of biographies, people are grouped according to their 'occupation, activity, pursuit and tribal affiliation. Categories are clustered under a few main headings, further broken down into subheadings'. There are minor variations of headings used; in volume three headings are: *armed forces, commercial activities, community service, construction and town-planning, education, health and welfare, land use, law and law enforcement, literature and scholarship, manufacturing and trades, marine, performing arts, politics, press, public administration, reform and protest, religion, science, service occupations, sport and recreation, transport, tribal affiliations, visual arts and crafts.*

The substantial 674-page first volume, containing biographies of nearly 600 people who first made their mark some time between 1769 and 1869, appeared in sesquicentennial year 1990. It was followed by the Maori-language volume, *Nga Tangata Taumata Rau*, 1769-1869, Wellington, 1990, containing translations of the 160 essays on Maori subjects, and a subsidiary volume, *The People of Many Peaks*, Wellington, 1991, a reprint in English of the essays which went into the Maori volume. Later came the illustrated *A People's History*, 1992, of biographies selected by W. H. Oliver, and — drawing now on two volumes of the main *Dictionary* — in 1993 for the centenary of the advent of universal suffrage, another illustrated book of selected biographies, *The Suffragists: Women Who Worked for the Vote.*

The publication schedule is expected to continue into the twenty-first century with English-language and Maori-language volumes covering the periods 1870-1900 (Volume two, published 1993), 1901-1920 (Volume three, 1996), 1921-1940 (Volume four, 1998), and 1941-1955 (Volume five), followed by a series of supplements for the period after 1955. Along with *Nga Tangata Taumata Rau*, the Maori-language Maori biographies, further subsidiary volumes have appeared, such as *The Turbulent Years*, 1994, the illustrated companion volume, in English, to *Nga Tangata Taumata Rau 1870-1900.* The wary user of the *Dictionary* material will quickly both appreciate the tremendous amount of scholarly output the project has generated, and the somewhat unexpected nature of the dates allocated to subjects (for example long-serving prime minister W. F. Massey — 1912-25 — appears in Volume two ending 1900, because he had begun his political career before the turn of the century). What may prove eventually to be one of the most beneficial results of the *Dictionary* project is the assembling of a considerable archive of material beyond that published, which is mounted in a database which will be maintained as a richly valuable permanent research facility. Another spin-off of the project is *Southern People*, the Otago-Southland 150th anniversary (1998) project of biographies from that region.

Arising from 'a desire to put together an alternative history — the history of the women in Aotearoa/New Zealand' is *The Book of New Zealand Women/Ko Kui Ma Te Kaupapa*, edited by Charlotte

Macdonald, Merimeri Penfold, and Bridget Williams, Wellington, 1991. The 300 or so women included range from the well known to others never known beyond their own immediate circle. Particularly useful is the detailed subject index. In addition to *The Suffragists* mentioned above, the 1993 edition of *The New Zealand Official Yearbook* [see **4.10**] also had a focus on women, as well as on women's issues. (For biographies of past and present women M.P.s see Janet McCallum, *Women in the House: Members of Parliament in New Zealand*, Picton, 1993, as well as the parliamentary *Who's Who* noted below.)

Scholefield's *Dictionary of New Zealand Biography* and the biographical entries in McLintock's *Encyclopaedia of New Zealand* [**4.2**] probably will always have some residual value since, despite its bulk, the modern *Dictionary of New Zealand Biography* has been less preoccupied with the Great and the Good than its predecessors. Scholefield's introduction also is useful for the outline it offers of pre-1940 biographical writing. Both Scholefield and McLintock, however, have omissions and factual mistakes — as of course do all reference works, but these perhaps rather more than some. Similarly, the old *Cyclopedia of New Zealand*, while it contains biographical details about a host of minor figures, is not entirely trustworthy — especially as contributors bought their placings.

From 1908, *Who's Who in New Zealand* (in its first four editions *Who's Who in New Zealand and the Western Pacific*), appearing at erratic intervals, has given brief biographies of a range of the living or recently dead. *Who's Who* also gives death notices of individuals listed in previous editions. Pioneered by G. H. Scholefield, who initiated many of our basic reference works, editions of *Who's Who* have appeared in 1908, 1924, 1932, 1941, 1951, 1956, 1961, 1964, 1968, 1971, 1978, and 1991. A rival *New Zealand Who's Who Aotearoa*, by Alister Taylor, first appeared in 1992. Initially perhaps treated by some subjects as a less prestigious work in which to be listed than the established *Who's Who*, new editions of Taylor's publication appeared in 1994 and 1996 and progressively it was able to match and in many ways exceed its rival in its comprehensive coverage. Alister Taylor is also publisher of the *Honoured by the Queen: New Zealand recipients of honours 1953-1993*. A second edition of *Debrett's Handbook of Australia and New Zealand*, ed. Dawn Henderson and James Orton, London and Sydney, was published in 1984. That same year the New Zealand Ministry of Foreign Affairs compiled for limited distribution a photocopied *Biographies of Members of the New Zealand Parliament*, their *Special bulletin* 1984/3, and since the 1987 election a triennial *New Zealand Parliament Who's Who* has been available, produced initially by the Parliamentary Service Commission, in 1996 by Radio New Zealand. Alister Taylor has produced *New Zealand Who's Who Parliamentary Directory, 1999*, a complete guide to central government. MPs' biographies also can be accessed on the Internet on the parliamentary service's website [www.ps.parliament.govt.nz].

For central government politics the most important printed publication for biographical information is the *New Zealand Parliamentary Record* [below **4.10**, and note further references there]. The *New Zealand Gazette* [**7.1.1**] not only notes public sector appointments but includes private sector personal information (teachers, medical practitioners, ministers of religion, bankrupts ...). From 1913 to 1946 the *New Zealand Gazette* published five-yearly listings of the entire public service, and similar lists were published for the Railways and Post and Telegraph departments. Some local authorities include lists of office holders in the handbooks, directories and diaries they publish for use of councillors, board members, and staff, and in their annual plans.

The Turnbull and several other research libraries have built up valuable biographical indexes, for example, Canterbury Museum's microfiche *Index to the George R. Macdonald Dictionary of Canterbury Biographies* (index, published in 1987, to the 10,500 biographies available on microfiche), and the New Zealand Women's Archives Collection, with over 5,000 entries, in the Auckland Institute and Museum. See the list of 'Working Files in Libraries' in the 1986 edition of A. P. U. Millett and F. T. H. Cole, *Bibliographical Work in New Zealand ...: Work in Progress and Work Published*, Hamilton, annual, 1980–. *New Zealand Electoral Rolls*, 1865-99, are available on microfiche in major libraries. Later rolls have been microfilmed by the Genealogical Society of Utah, of the Church of Jesus Christ of the Latter Day Saints (Mormons) and are held in some major libraries including the Turnbull. Also worth noting is H. E. M. Fildes, *Selective Indexes to Certain Books Relating to Early New Zealand*, Wellington, 1984, transcribed from the notebooks of a notable bibliophile, under four headings: Europeans, Maoris, Ships and Places. Through use of the indexes in the *Union Catalogue of New Zealand and Pacific Manuscripts in New Zealand Libraries*, interim edition, Wellington, l968-69, and the *National Register of Archives and Manuscripts* [**9.1**], it may be possible to trace references to persons, ships and places of interest to the biographer.

Genealogists have been active in seeking out, recording and publishing biographical sources. Many are produced by the New Zealand Society of Genealogists and listed in *The New Zealand Genealogist*. Of particular value are the *New Zealand Cemetery Records*, 1985–, on microfiche and updated irregularly. The main guides for genealogical research in New Zealand are:

Anne Bromell, *Tracing Family History in New Zealand*, rev. ed., Auckland, 1996, and the same author's

Tracing Family History Overseas from New Zealand, rev. ed., Auckland, 1991.

A guide on presentation for amateur genealogists is Joan Rosier-Jones, *Writing Your Family History*, Auckland, 1997. Sources at National Archives for genealogical and biographical research are described in greater detail in *Family History at National Archives*, Wellington, 1990, with an update: *Beyond the Book: an outline of genealogical sources at National Archives transferred or identified since the publication of Family history at National Archives*, Wellington, 1997. An example of the aids to which a librarian can direct a researcher is the microfiche *Index to Obituaries and Death Notices in the New Zealand Medical Journal 1886-February 1981*, compiled by D. G. Jamieson and Jocelyn Poland, Wellington, 1985, and published by the New Zealand Library Association. [On newspapers and newspaper indexes, see below, **6.2.**] Local government authorities are now putting their cemeteries' records on computer databases.

Of value to genealogists in particular is the vast quantity of biographical material accumulated by the Genealogical Society of Utah. For years, all over the globe, church workers have been photographing records useful for searching ancestors. Master copies are stored in a great vault in a granite mountain in Salt Lake City, and copies — microfilm or microfiche — can be obtained through any of the branch family history centres which are attached to the various Mormon chapels. From 1999 there is a genealogical web site: www.familysearch.org. New Zealand material aside, the richest and most obviously useful resource is a comprehensive coverage of British parish registers and censuses (cf. the microfiche 'International Genealogical Index'). There is for the library of the LDS (Latter Day Saints): *The Library: A Guide to the LDS Family History Library*, ed. John Cerny and Wendy Elliott, Salt Lake City, Utah, 1988.

Various lists and miscellaneous biographical information can be found in old almanacs — or in the case of the *Air New Zealand Almanac*, in a not-so-very-old publication [see below **4.6**]. And there are some specialist biographical compilations, for example of New Zealand criminals in *The Bad, the Very Bad, and the Ugly: Who's Who of NZ Crime*, by Tony Williams, 1998. John Clark, *Athletes at the Games*, 1998, gives brief biographies of the 86 New Zealand athletes who won medals at Olympic and Empire and Commonwealth Games, and Dorothy Simons has produced *New Zealand's Champion Sportswomen*, Auckland, 1982. Errol Martyn's *For Your Tomorrow: a record of New Zealanders who have died while serving with the RNZAF and Allied Air since 1915*, Christchurch, 1998, gives rank, a brief description of the action and any memorial on which the airmen are commemorated. Volume 1 goes up to 1942.

'In every part of the world where the history of English families excites any interest this book is well known and highly appreciated': thus a writer of 1906, quoted in 1967, on the famous G. W. Marshall, *The Genealogist's Guide*, 1st ed. 1879, 4th ed. 1903: reprinted Baltimore, 1967 with a new introduction by A. J. Camp. The *Guide* indexes local histories and periodicals and 'a multitude of out-of-the-way or forgotten books' (A. J. Camp). Marshall's work was continued, up to 1950, by J. B. Whitmore, compiler, *A Genealogical Guide*, London, 1953, and J. B. Barrow, compiler, *The Genealogist's Guide*, London, 1977.

Relations in Records: A Guide to Family History Sources in Australian Archives, Canberra, 1988, briefly outlines the history and functions of the Australian Archives and provides a guide to Commonwealth of Australia records held throughout Australia.

The Maori Land Court, now part of the Department of Courts, has substantial information on Maori genealogy. [Note **10.4.4** on Maori land.]

On the actual problems and techniques of biographical writing — especially, and perhaps discouragingly, on the problems — see *Biography in New Zealand*, edited by Jock Phillips, Wellington, 1985.

4.8 Business and commerce

For CD-ROM, online and Internet sources there is the detailed and extremely useful

> • *Electronic Sources of Information for Business in Australia and New Zealand*, by Tom Denison and Janet M. Stewart, 3rd. ed., 1998

which as well as a section on distributors and hosts, has 143 pages of sources.

Somewhat misleadingly entitled is the well-indexed *The New Zealand Business Who's Who,* 1935–, which gives no personal biographical details but lists all company directors and the companies they serve, as well as providing a comprehensive directory of New Zealand businesses along with such miscellaneous information as lists of central and local authorities and of diplomatic missions. For further business information, and for financial analysis of companies on the stock exchange register, see the *New Zealand Company Register*, Christchurch, 1962/63–. Databases include DATEX for company information [**2.2**], and the New Zealand Companies Office Database available from the Business and Registries branch of the Ministry of Commerce. As noted above [**4.4**], the Reserve Bank of New Zealand publishes its *Bulletin* and *Financial Statistics*.

4.9 Culture

An outstanding scholarly work, surveying the relatively new area of **print culture** is

• *Book & Print in New Zealand: A Guide to Print Culture in Aotearoa New Zealand*, edited by Penny Griffith, Ross Harvey and Keith Maslen, Wellington, 1997.

In this multi-authored volume contributors seek to explore the impact of various print forms on New Zealand culture, working through from the first printing of Maori material to the story of book production, publishing, distribution, holding, collecting and reading. There is even included a section on print culture of other languages. The bibliography is substantial and detailed.
The substantial

• *Oxford History of New Zealand Literature in English*, edited by Terry Sturm, now in its second edition (Auckland, 1998)

is an impressively inclusive work, ranging widely over our literary landscape — as one reviewer has put it — including Maori literature, non-fiction, popular fiction .... By way of contrast with this multi-author work, Patrick Evans's *The Penguin History of New Zealand Literature*, Auckland, 1990, is a lively and sometimes provocative solo performance (and is limited to 'literature' in the narrow sense of the word). Each chapter has full bibliographical notes. Along with its *History*, Oxford has also produced its *The Oxford Companion to New Zealand Literature*, edited by Roger Robinson and Nelson Wattie, Auckland, 1998, the essential guide to almost all New Zealand writers: a rich quarry, boasts its publisher, of information on 'writers and writing, and on the key movements that have influenced New Zealand's literary development'.

A much slighter work, *Three Hundred Years of New Zealand Books*, compiled by Peter Alcock and William Broughton, Palmerston North, 1990, is a select chronology, literary and general, with a commentary, of books published in or about New Zealand from Tasman to 1975. (The first title listed is John Ogilby's *America*, London, 1671, which included the first published account in English of Tasman's voyage.) A work by James Burns, *New Zealand Novels and Novelists 1861-1979: An Annotated Bibliography*, Auckland, 1981, a similar chronological listing, is more inclusive (within its stated field) and has author and title indexes.

Biographical and critical information about New Zealand writers is to be found in two valuable series: New Zealand Writers and their Work, published by Oxford University Press, and the Twayne's World Authors series. *Beginnings: New Zealand Writers Tell How They Began Writing*, ed. Robin Dudding, Wellington, 1980, brings together autobiographical essays originally commissioned for *Landfall* and *Islands*.

The work of major New Zealand dramatists, novelists and poets is included in the appropriate volume of the *Contemporary* series (*Contemporary Dramatists*,

The work of major New Zealand dramatists, novelists and poets is included in the appropriate volume of the *Contemporary* series (*Contemporary Dramatists*, 4th ed., Chicago, 1988, *Contemporary Novelists*, 4th ed., New York, 1986, *Contemporary Poets*, 6th ed., New York, 1996).

On writers specifically for children there are biographical sketches and accounts in: B. Gilderdale, *Introducing twenty-one New Zealand Children's Writers*, Auckland, 1991; Tom Fitzgibbon, *Beneath Southern Skies: New Zealand Children's Book Authors & Illustrators*, Auckland, 1993; Tom Fitzgibbon and Barbara Spiers ed., *Tea-trees and Iron Sands: A Guide to Present-day New Zealand Children's Writers*, Auckland, 1989; Tom Fitzgibbon and Barbara Spiers, *Matapihi: A Guide to Contemporary New Zealand Children's Book Illustrators*, Auckland, 1988.

There is some coverage of New Zealand literature in the *Annual Bibliography of English Language and Literature* and in the *MLA International Bibliography*, but the principal source is the 'Annual Bibliography of Commonwealth Literature: New Zealand', which has appeared in the *Journal of Commonwealth Literature* since 1964. *JNZL. Journal of New Zealand Literature* (1983–), carries annual surveys of recent New Zealand writing in the genres of poetry, the novel, short fiction and drama.

There is the framework for a bibliography and chronology of New Zealand **poetry** in the nearly-encyclopedic *Penguin Book of New Zealand Verse*, ed. Ian Wedde and Harvey McQueen, Auckland, 1985, with its chronological listing of poets (Maori and Pakeha) since about 1800, its select bibliography, several forms of index, plus introduction and notes. Mentioned above [1.2] was *An Anthology of New Zealand Poetry in English*, ed. Jenny Bornholdt, Gregory O'Brien and Mark Williams, Auckland, 1997.

Until recently few New Zealand **plays** were published, and it is not so easy to track down items still in manuscript. Peter Harcourt described in *Australasian Drama Studies* 18, April 1991, the discovery of more than thirty manuscripts (or synopses) of plays dating from 1886-1926, registered under the Copyright Law of 1877 with the Justice Department, and now deposited in the National Archives. There is discussion of published works in Howard McNaughton's *New Zealand Drama*, Boston, 1981, and *New Zealand Drama 1930-1980*, Auckland, 1984, by John E. P. Thomson.

An intriguing work, as yet only on disc, is Howard McNaughton's 'New Zealand Theatre Annals'. In the preservation of material relating to the history of theatre — perhaps the most ephemeral of all the arts — McNaughton's pioneering work provides an invaluable basis for further historical research. The Annals give a non-selective and non-evaluative listing of the records of productions, which may include extant advertisements, reviews, feature articles, programmes and publicity material. Researchers may contact Howard McNaughton through the English Department, University of Canterbury. A variety of sorting is available: there are frequent requests, for instance, to list the work of a particular director or playwright. For file structuring, entries are grouped according to one decade of one city's theatre. One example of a part-publication concentrating upon a certain period and place is *New Zealand Theatre Annals: Christchurch 1900-19*, Wellington, 1983. Almost completed is a published presentation collating South Island data from 1880 to 1980.

Playmarket, the script advisory service and playwrights agency, has published a list of published and unpublished play scripts of its clients, comprising the majority of playwrights working in New Zealand, as the *Playmarket Directory of NZ Plays and Playwrights 1985*, Wellington, 1985. Playmarket itself (P.O. Box 9767, Wellington) holds a certain amount of material on file relating to client authors: reviews, press releases, and so on, and research libraries hold articles such as scrapbooks of theatre reviews and programmes compiled by individuals and catalogued under their family name.

There have been two illustrated books on the subject of New Zealand theatre history: Peter Downes, *Shadows on the Stage: Theatre in New Zealand, The First 70 Years,* Dunedin, 1975; Peter Harcourt, *A Dramatic Appearance*, Wellington, 1978. Several theatres, such as Downstage (Wellington), the Court (Christchurch) and the Globe (Dunedin) have commissioned or been offered informal histories of their own; information regarding these materials, which often do not attain the status of books (the Court's 1991 anniversary retrospective was a glossy brochure), may be applied for through the theatres themselves.

On **art history**, Gil Docking's *Two Hundred Years of New Zealand Painting, with Additions by Michael Dunn Covering 1970-90*, revised edition, Auckland, 1990, and *An Introduction to New Zealand Painting 1839-1980*, by Gordon H. Brown and Hamish Keith, revised and enlarged edition, Auckland, 1982, are the principal works. Richard Dingwell, Rosemary Entwisle and Lois Robertson have edited *A Journal of Their Own: An Index to* Art in New Zealand*, 1928-1946, Bulletin of New Zealand Art History*, special series no. 2, 1997.

On specific themes are three historical surveys: Leonard Bell, *The Maori in European Art*, Wellington, 1980; Ian F. Grant, *The Unauthorized Version: A Cartoon History of New Zealand*, Auckland, 1980; Anne Kirker, *New Zealand Women Artists*, Auckland, 1986. *Early Prints of New Zealand 1642-1875*, by Enid and Don Ellis, Christchurch, 1978, which covers commercially produced plates, is an excellent guide to the pictorial complement of early exploring expeditions. Robin Kay and Tony Eden have written *Portrait of a Century: The History of the NZ Academy of Fine Arts 1882-1982*, Wellington, 1983. Focussing on a field somewhat neglected of late, Helen Schamroth has written *100 New Zealand craft artists*, Auckland, 1998.

Other art reference works are: Una Platt, *Nineteenth Century Artists: A Guide and Handbook*, Christchurch, 1980, and Max Germaine, *Artists and Galleries of Australia and New Zealand*, Sydney, 1979.

New Zealand Films 1912–1996, by Helen Martin and Sam Edwards, Auckland, 1997, starting with New Zealand's first feature

film, systematically lists films through the decades, with cast and crew where possible. A more broad overview work is *Celluloid Dreams: A Century of Film in New Zealand*, edited by Geoffrey Churchman, Stephen Cain and Patrick Hudson, 1997. There is a *New Zealand Film and Video Directory*, Auckland, 1987– (formerly *Film and Television Directory*, 1984–), and *The Brown Pages*, 3rd ed., Wellington, c1996, is a directory of Maori and Pacific people in the film, video and television industry.[See too **9.5**: Broadcasting and film, archives and manuscripts.]

Much of New Zealand culture has developed within the context of the broader British or European world. Hence, for example, brief introductory accounts of the history of **music** in New Zealand may be found in the articles on 'New Zealand' in the *New Grove Dictionary of Music and Musicians*, ed. Stanley Sadie, London, 1980 (see vol. 13, pp. 189-96), and in the *New Oxford Companion to Music*, ed. Denis Arnold, Oxford, 1983.

John Mansfield Thomson has produced the two major New Zealand reference works:

• *The Oxford History of New Zealand Music*, Auckland, 1991

and

• *Biographical Dictionary of New Zealand Composers*, Wellington, 1990

The Oxford History of New Zealand Music concentrates on European music from 1840 to 1990, but there is a preliminary chapter on Maori music by Te Puou Katene, and the book includes some account of music in the early years of European contact. Thomson treats his theme in two parts: firstly, the development of a performing tradition, and secondly, the development of a composing tradition. There are appendices on music education and instrument-making (the latter written by Justine Olsen and Len Stanners). The bibliography records the sources used, both published (books, articles, pamphlets and so on) and unpublished (manuscripts, theses).

Specialist works complementing *The Oxford History* include Philip Hayward, Tony Mitchell and Roy Shuker, *North Meets South: Popular Music in Aotearoa/New Zealand,* Sydney, 1994; John Dix, *Stranded in Paradise: New Zealand Rock'n'roll, 1955-1988,* Wellington, 1988 (described in *Crescendo*, April 1990, as 'the' book on the history of New Zealand rock music); Roger Watkins, *When Rock Got Rolling: The Wellington Scene, 1958-1970*, Christchurch, 1989; Roger Watkins, *Hostage to the Beat: The Auckland Scene, 1955-70,* North Shore City, 1995; Adrienne Simpson, *Opera's Farthest Frontier: a history of professional opera in New Zealand,* Auckland, 1996 (includes a substantial listing of bibliographical references), and the earlier Adrienne Simpson ed., *Opera in New Zealand: Aspects of History and Performance*, Wellington, 1990; Joy Tonks, *Bravo: The N. Z. S. O. at 50*, Auckland, 1996. There is unpublished *A Selected Annotated Discography of New Zealand Jazz Music held by the Alexander Turnbull Library*, Wellington, 1992.

Thomson's *Biographical Dictionary* has entries for over 100 New Zealand composers from the nineteenth century to the present day, and includes composers working in Britain and elsewhere as well as those resident in New Zealand. There are longer essays on the major figures, and the entries are followed by reference lists of 'works' (that is, compositions), 'writings' (by the composer), 'bibliography' (of writings about the composer), and, now and then, 'oral archives'. The composers themselves collaborated in the preparation of the entries, particularly in the selection of works to be listed. There are fifteen pages of appendices on musical organisations, publishing companies, and recording companies. Specifically on opera singers is *Southern Voices: International Opera Singers of New Zealand*, by Adrienne Simpson and Peter Downes, Auckland, 1992, with a similarly titled companion compact disc (1993).

There are a few older histories, mainly regional or institutional in character, such as Margaret Campbell (pseudonym of Ethel Anderson), *Music in Dunedin*, Dunedin, 1945; Brian Pritchard, *Words and Music: A Jubilee History of the Christchurch Harmonic Society*, Christchurch, 1977; John M. Jennings, *The Music Teaching Profession in New Zealand: A Jubilee History of the Music Teachers' Registration Board of New Zealand*, Wellington, 1978; John Mansfield Thomson, *Into a New Key: The Origins and History of the Music Federation of New Zealand Inc.*, Wellington, 1985.

Dorothy Freed's *Directory of New Zealand Music Organisations*, 2nd ed., Wellington, 1986, lists mainly voluntary organisations, giving their addresses, with the names of contact persons who can usually pass on inquiries made to them initially.

On sound recordings, one may consult: John M. Jennings, *Select List of New Zealand Compositions Published and/or Commercially Recorded*, Christchurch, 1988; Don McNaughtan, *Sound Recordings of New Zealand Popular Music: A checklist of 1165 LPs, EPs and cassettes recorded by New Zealand rock, jazz and folk musicians from 1958 to April 1987*, Wellington, 1989.

Indication of popular music played in New Zealand, mostly of overseas origin, is Warwick R. Freeman, *New Zealand Top 20 Singles*, Auckland, 1993, covering the years 1957-60 and 1966-93. Note also *Sounds Historical: A Catalogue of the Sound Recordings in the Sound Archives of Radio New Zealand*, Timaru, 1982 [below **9.5**, and see also **Finding Maori Information: 10.4.2.**]

4.10   Official

The main printed source for most official material in the broadest sense is the (almost) annual

• *New Zealand Official Yearbook,*

first published in 1893. Previously there had been occasional *Official Handbooks*, the first of which was compiled by Julius Vogel and published in London in 1875. A new handbook was issued by F. D. Bell in London in 1883/4, and in 1889 and 1890 handbooks were produced by the New Zealand Registrar-General (forerunner of Statistics New Zealand). Much expanded in 1892, it was next year retitled *Official Year-Book*; it has been *Yearbook* since 1961. This splendid compendium of knowledge provides an overview of New Zealand through more than a century and while each successive edition updates its predecessor it does not supersede it: the series stands as a full set.

• J. B. Ringer, *An Introduction to New Zealand Government,* Christchurch, 1991

bristles with information on government, how it operates and what is published. More recent is the booklet by C. L. Carpenter, 1994, Part V of the *Guide to New Zealand Information Sources* [referred to above 4.1], and an intended annual: *New Zealand Government Directory,* Sydney, Auckland, Wellington, 1997, is a comprehensive guide covering the New Zealand system of government.
New Zealand Government Online is at

• http://www.govt.nz.

Government departments — as well as parliament and the political parties — have their own websites on the Internet. Current political office holders, along with all Members of Parliament and their party affiliations and select committee membership, also are listed in the *Parliamentary Debates* [below 7.1.2].
For past parliamentary and governmental details, reference should be made to the *New Zealand Parliamentary Record 1840-1984,* ed. J. O. Wilson, Wellington, 1985, and earlier editions for provincial councils, and to *Ministers and Members in the New Zealand Parliament,* ed. G. A. Wood, Dunedin, 1996. Both Wilson and Wood track the various major and minor reshuffles of ministerial posts.
Since 1879 parliamentary **election** results have been published in full in the *Appendices to the Journals of the House of Representatives* in the year following an election (as papers H. 33 and H. 33A after 1914, and E.9 since 1973). Historical statistics for the post-war years are collected by Clifford Norton in *New Zealand Parliamentary Elections: 1946-1987,* Wellington, 1988. Until recent years, official publication of by-election results was erratic: some may be found in the *New Zealand Gazette* or *Appendices to the Journals* or

(unofficially) in the *Yearbook*. Before 1958 official returns did not give candidates' party affiliations; the simplest way to find these for the previous half-century is to look up election results in *Who's Who*. (Note that not all elections are covered, and the party labels of some minor candidates are in dispute.)

For details of results before 1879 it is necessary to search through newspaper reports; for local and regional results such search may be unavoidable for the twentieth century as well as for the nineteenth, although every local authority should hold electoral records (if without party accreditations until the 1970s). Statistics relating to local body elections (1959–) have been published in increasingly stylish and interesting form by the Department of Internal Affairs: *Local Authority Election Statistics*, 1967–, although some patience may be called for in awaiting information on the most recent triennial local elections.

General electorate boundaries were described in a government proclamation of 1853 [see on the *New Zealand Gazette*, below **7.1.1**], revised in subsequent Electoral Districts (1858) and Representation (1860–) Acts, put in the hands of Representation Commissions (reports in the *Appendices to the Journals of the House of Representatives*, 1891–), and shown on publicly issued Commission maps (accompanying reports, 1911–). Maori electorate boundaries before 1981 were published in the *New Zealand Gazette* (1868, 1919, 1951, 1954). Alan McRobie's detailed *New Zealand Electoral Atlas*, Wellington, 1989 [above **4.5**], aims to give the location and extent of every electorate in New Zealand since 1853.

4.11 Science

Official organised science in New Zealand dates back to 1861, and appointment as Canterbury provincial geologist of Julius von Haast (the subject of one of New Zealand's most substantial *Life and Times*, written by his son H. F. von Haast, Wellington, 1948). In the following decades various scientific units were set up in the public sector until in 1926 a number were merged into a new Department of Scientific and Industrial Research. While other government departments maintained their own research divisions, such as in agriculture, until the early 1990s, and apart from the universities, the Department of Scientific and Industrial Research was the principal agency promoting and organising scientific research in New Zealand as well as a major publisher of scientific information. In 1990 the Ministry of Research, Science and Technology was established, to be government's principal policy adviser, along with a Foundation for Research, Science and Technology to allocate research funds. In 1992 the Department of Scientific and Industrial Research was disestablished and its functions along with science agencies in agriculture, meteorology, forestry and communicable diseases were transferred into nine new crown-owned research institutes: Forest Research, AgResearch, HortResearch, NZ Institute for Crop and Food Research Ltd, Landcare Research New Zealand Ltd, Institute of Geological and Nuclear Sciences Ltd, Industrial Research Ltd—IRL, NIWA (National Institute of Water and Atmospheric Research Ltd), Institute of Environmental Science and Research Ltd—ESR. Outline of functions, websites, and a description of the science system in New Zealand is provided in *The New Zealand Official Yearbook.* The Ministry of Research, Science and Technology also has produced a booklet *The Science System in New Zealand,* 2nd rev. ed., Wellington, 1994.

The Foundation has published a slim *Nationally Significant Public Good Science Fund Databases and Collections,* Wellington, 1993. Some of these databases are available on the Knowledge Basket [www.knowledge-basket.co.nz, **2.2**], giving access to catalogues, bibliographies, articles, abstracts, and indexes of journals, and including the database of the former Department, now available as New Zealand Science, formerly STIX. Produced by one of the Department's successor agencies — Industrial Research Ltd — New Zealand Science has indexes to major science journals and various informal and unpublished reports, and catalogues and abstracts from papers and monographs. Other databases, produced by the Institute of Geological and Nuclear Sciences, include GEOBIB, a bibliography of geology along with articles from newsletters and newspapers; GEOPUB, a publications catalogue of geological and geophysical titles (— books, reports, maps, brochures, photographs, and postcards).

Statistics New Zealand's *Environmental Directory: databases and collections,* loose leaf, Wellington, 1996– [noted above **4.1**], is compiled from entries supplied by holding organisations, and takes a very broad view of 'environmental' subjects.

The Patent Office in the Ministry of Commerce publishes its *New Zealand Patent Office Journal* : early patents were published in the *New Zealand Gazette.*

Sir Charles Fleming's *Science, Settlers, and Scholars: The Centennial History of the Royal Society of New Zealand,* Wellington, 1987, is the principal source for the history of science in New Zealand. See the Preface (p. xi), and the references there cited, for the works on which it builds — some accounts by historians of science (I. D. Dick, M. E. Hoare), articles in *An Encyclopaedia of New Zealand,* ed. A. H. McLintock, 1966, various institutional histories, and biographies and obituaries of individuals. The list of references (pp. 337-45) is, in effect, a bibliography of the history of science in New Zealand. (There is also a brief history of science in the 1967 edition of the *New Zealand Official Yearbook.*)

The Royal Society of New Zealand maintains a database of scientists, technologists and people with an interest in New Zealand science. (The Society has its own website, www.rsnz.govt.nz.)

'Science' is also one of the many groups identified in the Categories Index of *The Dictionary of New Zealand Biography.*

4.12 Statistics

The Victorian love of statistics ensured that from earliest days of British colonisation New Zealand statistics were being collected. Thanks to the scope offered by databases that love by the 1990s has become perhaps a passion. Statistics New Zealand [www.stats.govt.nz], the major compiler and generator of statistical information, has its database INFOS, for which since 1985 it has produced guides and indexes, latterly as *Data Directory: your computer guide to the INFOS database,* Wellington, 1991–, and *INFOS index of the database,* Wellington, 1995–. [See, too, Subject bibliographies, **5.3.1:** Statistics.] In the late 1980s as the department moved to operate on a net-funding basis, its role changed and it expanded beyond production of 'public good' statistics to providing a range of customised statistics and services. Symbolic of the change, from 1989, after three quarters of a century, the 'Monthly Abstract of Statistics' ceased publication to be replaced by the new monthly *Key Statistics,* still intended to provide up-to-date, shorter-term economic and demographic statistics. In addition, a stream of statistical information is issued through the year in the 'Hot off the Press' series.

While Statistics New Zealand remains by far the most significant source of all official statistics, dating back, through work of the department's predecessors, to the earliest day of European government in New Zealand, there are a number of departments and agencies in the business of statistics collection — in justice, health, elections, policing, customs, welfare, business and finance ...

The most impressive treasure trove of New Zealand statistics is the information about population and dwellings gathered in the quinquennial **censuses** — latest held 1996 — which generate a range of publications (education, electoral profile, families and households, incomes ...) along with material accessible on the Statistics database and on CD-ROM (— Supermap 3 for example, with a users guide provided, comprises data from the 1996 census and some tables of data from 1991 and 1986 along with mapping information, to enable analysis and mapping of the census results). The first New Zealand-wide census, restricted, however, to non-Maori, was held in 1851. Previously figures had been gathered in the several small settlements for the annual handwritten (in triplicate) 'Blue Books' required by the British Colonial Office, copies of which are held in the National Archives. There is, however, *Statistics of New Zealand for the Crown Colony Period, 1840-1852,* Auckland University College Department of Economics, 1955. From 1858 censuses were held at three or four year intervals until 1881, since when a five-yearly sequence has been interrupted only by the Depression and the second world war. A census of New Zealand Maori was taken in 1858, and then from 1874 censuses were held more or less contemporaneously with the non-Maori. From 1951 one comprehensive census has been held for all present in New Zealand on census night.

Census results are published — but not by an organisation familiar with the trials of a library catalogue user. So, although 'New Zealand Census of Population and Dwellings' may turn up a number of references, search may have to extend to 'Results of a Census ...' , 'Census of New Zealand', Dominion of New Zealand Population Census', 'New Zealand Population Census', or today's 'Census 1996'. Once statistical information had been extracted, census forms were destroyed (unlike United Kingdom, Canada, United States, for example, where census forms over one hundred years old now are available). Latterly, however, since 1966 forms from alternate censuses have been retained to be viewable after one hundred years.

Fortunately various packagings of statistics are available, most notably

• David C. Thorns and Charles P. Sedgwick, *Understanding Aotearoa/New Zealand: Historical Statistics*, Palmerston North, 1997

— a useful, and intriguing, compilation of tables, graphs and figures, along with commentary, ranging through population data, to economic, social and political.

The New Zealand volume in an American International Statistics series, *New Zealand: A Handbook of Historical Statistics,* by G. T. Bloomfield, Boston, Massachusetts, 1984, covers education, justice, production, trade, transport ... — almost every topic likely to be of relevance to the researcher. Also to be noted is B. L. Evans, *Agricultural and Pastoral Statistics of New Zealand 1861-1954*, Wellington, 1956. Statistics on the sheep and wool industry have been published since 1950 by the New Zealand Wool Commission and its successor bodies (since 1978 in the New Zealand Wool Board's *Statistical Handbook*, Wellington). Each year a mass of financial statistics is published in association with the annual budget exercise and published in the *Appendices to the Journals of the House of Representatives.*

On the Maori population of New Zealand, note especially Ian Pool, *Te Iwi Maori: A New Zealand Population, Past, Present & Projected*, Auckland, 1991.

The journal, *New Zealand Population Review*, Wellington, 1972–, has articles on the demography of New Zealand and the South Pacific, together with research notes, comments and reviews.

[On financial statistics note **4.4** above, and on elections **4.10**.]

4.13 Australian and British reference material

[See too 5.1 National bibliographies]

D. H. Borchardt's *Australian Bibliography: A Guide to Printed Sources of Information*, Rushcutters Bay, 1976, is outstanding. The great **Australian** biographical work is the *Australian Dictionary of Biography*, ed. Douglas Pike et al., Melbourne, 1966–. So far, fourteen volumes have been published, covering 1788 to 1939 (vols 1-2: 1788-1850; vols 3-6: 1851-1890; vols 7-12: 1891-1939, with a separate index, vol. 13). Further volumes, for the years 1940-1981, are planned. The major Australian encyclopedia is *The Australian Encyclopaedia*, 4th ed., 12 vols, Sydney, 1983.

It is a quirk of history that in lexicography in the English language New Zealanders have been to the fore; even *The Australian National Dictionary: a dictionary of Australianisms on historical principles*, Melbourne, 1988, is edited by a Wellington graduate, W. S. Ramson. Following that dictionary's publication the Australian National Dictionary Centre was established by Oxford University Press and the Australian National University with responsibility for producing Oxford's several Australian dictionaries.

Oxford University Press has in fact produced a number of major regional dictionaries which complement its 20-volume *Oxford English Dictionary*, 2nd ed., 1989. In addition to the Australian and New Zealand dictionaries are a South African dictionary (1996) and Canadian (1998).

The wealth of **British** reference material is too great even for a summary. The more obviously indispensable British works, in addition to the *Oxford English Dictionary*, are the great encyclopedias: *Encyclopaedia Britannica*, 1768-71– (a British publication until 1929) and *Chambers's Encyclopaedia*, 1850-68–. As well as the occasional new edition, over the years the encyclopedias published year-books (as *Britannica Book of the Year*, and *Chambers's Encyclopaedia World Survey*). Today, for such reference works traditional forms of publication have very largely been overtaken by electronic ware. For example in 1997 the *Encyclopaedia Britannica* released one CD-ROM, instead of 32 solid printed volumes: in response to a typed question the *Encyclopaedia* will provide answers, and it offers links to other relevant entries (—although these cannot always be found or, if found, prove relevant). It is possible, too, to connect with Britannica Online, a reference site on the Internet. For less instantly up-to-date information, but handy for chronological summaries and general information are works such as *Pears Cyclopaedia: a book of background information and reference*, London, 1897– and [noted above, **4.4**] *The Annual Register*.

In addition, among the major works are: *The Dictionary of National Biography*, edited by Sir L. Stephen and Sir S. Lee, London,

1908-9, 22 vols plus later *Supplements* (corrections to which are published in the *Bulletin of the Institute of Historical Research*), with new edition planned; *Who's Who*; an annual biographical dictionary, London, 1849–; The *New Cambridge Bibliography of English Literature*, Cambridge, 1969–; *The Times*, London, *Times Atlas of the World. Mid-Century edition*, London, 1955-59, 5 vols — hopelessly out of date for political names and boundaries, of course. (But as noted above [2.2] updated material is available on CD-ROM or through the Internet.)

5. Bibliographies

The arts, literature, theatre and music
Children's books
Commissions and inquiries
Economics and economic history
Education
Environment
External relations
Family
Health and welfare
History
Immigration
Labour and industrial relations

Law
Military
Natural history
Politics
Regional studies
Religion
Science
Sexuality and gender studies
Social Science
Sport and Recreation
Statistics
Tourism
Women's studies

5.1 National bibliographies

As already noted, major bibliographies are now available on the Internet.

Two established major bibliographies for English-speaking students, with author, title, and subject entries have been:

- *Cumulative Book Index: a world list of books in the English Language*, New York, 1898–, print and CD-ROM, annual

- *British National Bibliography: A Subject Catalogue of New British books received by the Copyright Receipt Office of the British Library,* London, 1950–.

Both are available online, *British National Bibliography* as BNBMARC database. The British Library catalogue can be searched at http://minos.bl.uk/index.html.

5.1.1 New Zealand

J. E. Traue's *New Zealand Studies: A Guide to Bibliographic Resources*, Wellington, 1985, is a gracefully written and helpful essay, concentrating on bibliographies and finding aids for the printed, the unprinted, the recorded and the pictured.

As mentioned above [**1.1**], for many years the *New Zealand Official Yearbook* each year included a bald, but sometimes handy selected list of books on all aspects of New Zealand, and particularly of books in print at the time, giving a bird's eye view of New Zealand studies through the decades. The *Yearbooks* for 1932, 1947/9 and 1961 list, respectively, works published before 1932, 1912-49, and 1950-61. The series ended in 1990 when the *Yearbook* went more up-market for the New Zealand sesquicentenary.

The basic, fully indexed and detailed list of New Zealand books and pamphlets is the

* *New Zealand National Bibliography to the year 1960*, ed. A. G. Bagnall, 5 vols in 6, Wellington, 1969 [1970]-1985:

a magnificent achievement, and finally a replacement for T. M. Hocken's notable *A Bibliography of the Literature relating to New Zealand*, Wellington, 1909 (reprinted, 1973). Working at a time before periodical indexes were available, Hocken also included a selective listing of periodical articles. Many of the titles listed in Hocken and Bagnall are, of course, rare and difficult to obtain, and libraries and other organisations have for some years been making microform copies so that they may be more readily accessible to researchers. [See too **Finding Maori Information: 10.4.1.**] A. P. U. Millett's compilation *Publications Republished in Microform: a bibliography*, Hamilton, 1989, gave a convenient listing of titles so copied.

The Turnbull Library's New Zealand and Pacific catalogue on microfiche — one set of 488 fiche listing authors and titles and another set of 308 fiche listing subjects — is a rich source for New Zealand books and pamphlets and contains many items considered out of scope by Bagnall.

For the period since 1960 New Zealand is reasonably well served. The

* *New Zealand National Bibliography* (after 1983 on microfiche; accessible on Te Puna as previously on the New Zealand Bibliographic Network, and also in monthly paper issues),

lists all publications either produced in New Zealand or having New Zealand relevance. Entries are not dissimilar to entries in a library's online catalogue [discussed above **3.3**]. The *National Bibliography* includes maps, pamphlets, music, annual publications, and new serials. There are two main sequences: author/title and subject. The *New Zealand National Bibliography* replaced the *Current National Bibliography*, Wellington, 1940-1966, an annual list of monographs which included subject entries, and *Copyright Publications*, Wellington, 1949-1965, which listed, by author only, publications deposited in the General Assembly (Parliamentary) Library under the then Copyright Act. (As noted above [**3.1**], today the legal deposit office is in the National Library, and requirement to deposit (three copies of) all publications is enacted in the National Library Act.)

Pamphlets are not the easiest items to find, yet can be said to represent the undergrowth of printed comment and debate. There are detailed catalogues of some of the main, old, collections. From the Parliamentary Library, formerly General Assembly Library, is *General Assembly Library, Alphabetical List of the Bound Pamphlets in the General Assembly Library ...*, 44 vols, Wellington, 1890, and other notable nineteenth century collections: W. H. Trimble, *Catalogue of the Hocken Library*, Dunedin, 1912; Augustus Hamilton, *List of the Pamphlets Bound up in the Eighty-three Volumes in the C. R. Carter Collection now in the Library of the Dominion Museum and the New Zealand Institute, Wellington,* Wellington, 1911. As noted above, the Dominion Museum, later National Museum, is now, of course transformed into Te Papa, or MONZ, the Museum of New Zealand.

Victoria University of Wellington Library has published: H. E. M. Fildes, *Selective Indexes to Certain Books Relating to Early New Zealand,* Wellington, 1984 [cited above, **4.7**]; see also K. A. Coleridge, 'Horace Fildes and his collection', *New Zealand Libraries* 38 (1975): 254-69; Victoria University of Wellington, *The Pamphlet Collection of Sir Robert Stout: A Catalogue with Indexes*, compiled and edited by K. A. Coleridge, Wellington, 1987. (An earlier guide to these two Victoria University collections is I. M. Winchester's *A Study of Two Special New Zealand Collections: The Fildes Collection and the Sir Robert Stout Collection of New Zealand Pamphlets at the Victoria University of Wellington*, Wellington, 1961.)

There is a compilation of New Zealand pamphlets in the *Subject Catalogue of the Library of the Royal Empire Society* and *Subject Catalogue of the Royal Commonwealth Society* [below **5.2**].

5.1.2 Australia

The standard bibliography of nineteenth-century Australian literature is J. A. Ferguson, *Bibliography of Australia, 1784-1900*, Sydney, 1941-69, which is comparable to New Zealand's *Hocken Bibliography*. A reprint of Ferguson has been issued by the National Library of Australia, together with a new volume, *Addenda 1784-1850* (*Volumes I to IV*), Canberra, 1986. For modern Australian publications the main guide is the *Australian National Bibliography*, Canberra, 1961– (together with the earlier *Annual Catalogue of Australian Publications*, Canberra, 1936-60). The gap between Ferguson and the current *Australian National Bibliography* (*A. N. B.*) has recently been filled by the retrospective *Australian National Bibliography, 1901-1950*, 4 vols, Canberra, 1988.

5.2 Published library catalogues

Major library catalogues are online and accessible through the Internet. As well, still on many library shelves will be found the old solid printed volumes. A comprehensive annual index of publications from 1950 through 1983 is to be found in the *Subject Catalog* of the Library of Congress of the United States (the title varies), continued on microfiche as the monthly *NUC Books*, Washington, 1983–, with annual and longer period cumulations.

Also valuable for bibliographical searching are the printed catalogues of some major research libraries overseas. In **Australia** there is

>Library of New South Wales. Mitchell Library, *Dictionary Catalog of Printed Books*, Boston, 1969, 38 vols, and *First Supplement*, 1970.

The Mitchell is probably the most important Australasian research library. For a brief history of the Library of New South Wales, see G. D. Richardson, 'The Colony's Quest for a National Library', *Journal and Proceedings of the Royal Australian Historical Society*, 47 (1961-62): 61-93. Sets of the Mitchell Library's *Dictionary Catalog* are held in several major libraries — such as the Turnbull Library and the libraries of the Universities of Auckland and Otago. The Mitchell is also producing a catalogue of its manuscripts [see below **9.7**]. In addition, collections of personal and private archives housed in that library are described in a number of in-house finding aids and a number of detailed Guides have been published in hard copy. (For details see the Mitchell page on the website of the New South Wales library — www.slnsw.gov.au.)

In **Great Britain**:

>Great Britain. Colonial Office. Library. *Catalogue of the Colonial Office Library*, 15 vols, London and Boston, 1964

>Royal Commonwealth Society, London. Library. *Subject Catalogue of the Library of the Royal Empire Society, formerly Royal Colonial Institute*, by P. Evans Lewin, 4 vols, London, 1930-37, reprinted 1967 (vol. 1: British Empire ...; vol. 2: Australia, New Zealand, South Pacific ...), and its sequel, *Subject Catalogue of the Royal Commonwealth Society*, 7 vols, Boston, Massachusetts, 1971 (vol. 1: British Commonwealth ...; vol. 6: Australia, New Zealand, Pacific). There is also a one-volume *Biography Catalogue of the Library of the Royal Commonwealth Society*, London, 1961

>City of London Polytechnic, *Biblio Fem*, a catalogue of the Polytechnic's Fawcett Library and of the library of the U.K. Equal Opportunities Commission plus other bibliographic information; it is said to be 'the

premier updating and reference source on every aspect of women all over
the world'.

5.3 New Zealand subject bibliographies

Over the years a progressively ever larger number of scholarly, or at
least serious non-fiction, books has been published in New Zealand—
more material for a researcher to track down, but an aid also to that
task, for some books include substantial and well laid-out
bibliographies. For focused search, and for guidance into the material,
these may be more immediately helpful than broader electronic
searching — at least in the first instance.

For a broad and descriptive range of New Zealand works,
ordered by subject and well indexed, there is a revised volume 18 in
the Clio Press World Bibliographical Series

- *New Zealand*, rev. ed., compiled by Brad Patterson and
  Kathryn Patterson, Oxford, 1998

A guide to specialised subject bibliographies is provided by A.
P. U. Millett and F. T. H. Cole, *Bibliographical Work in New
Zealand ...: Work in Progress and Work Published*, Hamilton, annual,
1980–, a continuation of 'Bibliographical work in progress' which
appeared irregularly in *New Zealand Libraries* between 1962 and
1977. For older material there is the New Zealand Library
Association's publication, *A Bibliography of New Zealand
Bibliographies*, preliminary ed., Wellington, 1967.

For bibliographies compiled by students of the old New Zealand Library
School see Anne H. Rimmer and William A. Siddells, *A Bibliography of New
Zealand Library School Bibliographies 1946-1972*, Wellington, 1972, and its
supplement by Margaret A. Pay and K. J. Cunningham issued in 1977.

5.3.1 Printed subject bibliographies: a selected list

The arts, literature,
    theatre and music
Children's books
Commissions and
    inquiries
Economics and
    economic history
Education
Environment
External relations
Family
Health and welfare
History
Immigration

Labour and industrial
    relations
Law
Military
Natural history
Politics
Regional studies
Religion
Science
Sexuality and gender
    studies
Social Science
Sport and Recreation

Statistics   Women's studies
Tourism

The following are some of the more obviously useful specialised bibliographies; generally the most up-to-date or most useful are listed first.

The arts, literature, theatre and music

> *Oxford History of New Zealand Literature in English*, ed. Terry Sturm, Auckland, 1991, pp. 603-709 (a revision and updating of John E. P. Thomson, *New Zealand Literature to 1977: A Guide to Information Sources*, Detroit, 1980).

Peter and Diane Beatson, *The Arts in Aotearoa New Zealand: Themes and Issues*, Palmerston North, 1994, pp. 265–270.

Books & Pamphlets relating to Culture and the Arts in New Zealand: A Bibliography Including Works Published to the End of the Year 1977, compiled by Bernard W. Smyth and Hilary Howorth, Christchurch, 1978. [See too **Finding Maori Information: 10.4.2**]

Norman Simms, *Writers from the South Pacific: a Bio-bibliographical critical encyclopaedia.*, Washington, 1991, *Part II Who's who: supplement.* Working draft 12, February 1993 [See too **10.4.2.**]

Nicholas J. Goetzfridt, *Indigenous Literature of Oceania: A survey of criticism and interpretation.* Westport, 1995. [See too **10.4.2.**]

Howard McNaughton's *New Zealand Drama*, Boston, 1981, has a five page bibliography.

Philip Norman, compiler, *Bibliography of New Zealand Compositions*, vol. 1, 3rd ed., Christchurch, 1991 (lists over 3000 New Zealand compositions available for performance, indexed primarily by medium, and gives such details as date, title, voices and/or instrumentation, duration, and location of scores).

Mike Harding, *When the Pakeha Sings of Home: A Source Guide to the Folk and Popular Songs of New Zealand*, Auckland, 1992.

D. R. Harvey, compiler, *A Bibliography of Writings about New Zealand Music Published to the End of 1983*, Wellington, 1985.

see too *The Oxford History of New Zealand Music*, Auckland, 1991 [above **4.9**].

Dorothy Freed and Gerald Seaman, *Orchestral Scores: A New Zealand Finding List of performing editions with parts, available on loan from some New Zealand musical societies and libraries*, 2nd ed., Wellington, 1984.

Brian W. Pritchard, *Sing! A Catalogue of Choral Scores in Multiple Copies held by New Zealand musical organisations, societies and libraries*, Wellington, 2nd ed., 1995.

D. R. Harvey, *Music at National Archives: Sources for the study of music in New Zealand*, Christchurch, 1991 (no. 5 in the *Canterbury Series of Bibliographies, Catalogues and Source Documents in Music*: University of Canterbury School of Music, 1984–).

Robert Petre, *A Bibliography of Printed Music Published before 1801, Held in the Rare Book Room and Bishop's House Collection in the Auckland Public Library*, Auckland, 1977.

Elizabeth F. Nichol, 'Printed Music Published before 1800: A Bibliography of the Holdings of some Wellington Libraries', unpublished Library School bibliography, Wellington, 1979.

Children's books

Mary C. Austin and Ester C. Jenkins, *Literature for Children and Young Adults about Oceania: analysis and annotated bibliography with additional readings for adults* (no. 49 in Bibliographies and Indexes in World Literature), Westport, 1996.

Betty Gilderdale, *A Sea Change: 145 Years of New Zealand Junior Fiction*, Auckland, 1982.

Diane Hebley, *Off the Shelf: twenty one years of New Zealand books for children*, Auckland, 1980.

Commissions and inquiries

Evelyn Robertson and Peter H. Hughes (compilers), *A Checklist: New Zealand Royal Commissions, Commissions and Committees of Inquiry 1864-1981*, with additional entries by Dorothy Henderson, Wellington, 1982.

David C. Thorns and Charles P. Sedgwick, *Understanding Aotearoa/New Zealand: Historical Statistics*, Palmerston North, 1997, pp. 186-190.

As the inquiries of highest status, royal commissions may both contain a mass of accumulated material and act as a point of reference for later public policy decisions. See, for example, reports of commissions on Cost of Living (1912), University Education (1925), Licensing (1946), Gaming and Racing (1948), Monetary, Banking, and Credit Systems (1956), Electoral System (1986). Reports normally appear in the *Appendices to the Journals of the House of Representatives* — but not necessarily so. A useful booklet, produced for the use of commissioners, is *Royal Commissions and Commissions of Inquiry*, Wellington, 1974.

Culture see *The Arts, literature, theatre and music* above

Demography see *Statistics*

Economics and economic history

Simon P. Ville, *A Select Bibliography of the Business History of New Zealand*, Auckland, 1993.

Nancy Wilson and Alan Bollard, compilers, *A Bibliography of New Zealand Industrial Economics Research*, Wellington, 1984.

C. N. Taylor, C. Bettesworth and J. G. Kerslake, *Social Implications of Rapid Industrialisation: A Bibliography of New Zealand Experiences*, Christchurch, 1983.

R. H. Carey and F. W. Holmes, compilers, *A Preliminary Bibliography of New Zealand Economics and Economic History*, Wellington, 1967.

G. M. Reid, A. G. Matheson, G. M. Walton, *Bibliography of New Zealand Apiculture, 1842-1986*, Tauranga, 1988.

Wool Research Organisation of New Zealand, *Publications for the Wool Industry, 1963-1991*, Christchurch, [1992].

Reserve Bank of New Zealand, *Bibliography of Banking and Currency in New Zealand*, reprinted from the *Reserve Bank Bulletin*, June 1968.

Note also the bibliography in G. R. Hawke, *The Making of New Zealand: An Economic History*, Cambridge, 1985.

As noted above, **4.8**, increasingly commercial and business information may be accessed on the Internet and on CD-ROM.

Education

Guide to New Zealand Information Sources, Part III: Education, compiled by L. E. Battye [Marsden], Palmerston North, 1978.

R. Boshier, *Adult and Continuing Education in New Zealand, 1851-1978: A Bibliography*, Vancouver, 1979.

Elizabeth Wagner, compiler, *Continuing Education, Bibliography, 1970-1990: information on continuing education publications not readily found in nationally accessible databases*, Wellington, 1990.

NZCER 1934-1984: The Published Record: A Bibliography, compiled by Elaine Marland and Keith Pickens, Wellington, 1985.

Keith Pickens et al., *Gifted and Talented Children: a bibliography of the New Zealand documentation; a joint project,* Wellington, 1992.

H. O. Roth, *A Bibliography of New Zealand Education*, Wellington, 1964.

Environment

Guide to New Zealand Information Sources, Part VII: Geography, compiled by B. A. Allan, Palmerston North, 1982.

Nancy Ellis, compiler, *The New Zealand Environment: A Bibliography ... 1968-1974*, Wellington, Nature Conservation Council, 1975, with seven *Supplements* (1976-85) covering material published up to 1982. A further *Supplement* for 1983-84 was published in 1986 by the National Water and Soil Conservation Authority.

P. A. Memon & G. A. Wilson, *Recent Indigenous Forest Policy Issues in New Zealand: an annotated bibliography*, Dunedin, 1992. (Encompasses the period 1970-1991.)

Environmental Education Support Group, *Environmental Resource Directory: directory of resource material available for environmental education*, [loose leaf], Christchurch, 1995.

> New Zealand. Ministry of Works and Development. Town and Country Planning Directorate, *Planning Research Index, 1969-84* gave annual listing and abstracts of papers and books concerned with people and their interaction with the social, economic and physical aspects of the environment; there is a Planning Research Index: Master Index 1969-1981.

> [Note also Statistics New Zealand, *Environmental Directory: databases and collections* [**4.1**], and **7.1.3**: law reports (— resource management). For its internal use the Department of Conservation's science and research directorate has produced Bev James, *The Use of DOC Science and Research Publications*, Wellington, c1991.]

External relations

Malcolm McKinnon, *Independence and Foreign Policy: New Zealand in the World Since 1935*, Auckland, 1993, has a useful bibliography.

Beyond New Zealand: The Foreign Policy of a Small State, ed. J. Henderson, K. Jackson and R. Kennaway, Auckland, 1980, had a 'guide to further reading' to which *Beyond New Zealand II*, ed. Richard Kennaway and John Henderson, Auckland 1991, adds an update. A more extended list was published by the New Zealand Institute of International Affairs as *New Zealand Foreign Policy 1948-1985: A Bibliography*, Wellington, 1986. The New Zealand Institute of International Affairs has published a number of booklets, and some books, over a period of years, and the proceedings of a number of University of Otago foreign policy schools (from 1966 on) have also been published.

> J. Caudwell, 'New Zealand and the European Economic Community: A Select Bibliography', unpublished Library School bibliography, Wellington, 1972.

Family

(see also *Women's Studies*)
P. G. Koopman-Boyden, *A Bibliography of the New Zealand Family*, Christchurch, 1975 (covering such topics as birth, marriage, economics of the family, and so on, for the years 1857 to 1974), and *New Zealand Families: A Bibliography 1975-1980*, Christchurch, 1982.

Health and welfare

(see also *Statistics*)

Derek A. Dow, compiler, *Annotated Bibliography for the History of Health and Medicine in New Zealand*, Dunedin, 1994.

Patricia A. Sargison, *From Candles to Computers: A Bibliography of Printed Sources on the History of Nursing in New Zealand*, Wellington, 1986.

Natasha Glaisyer, Jane Chetwynd, and Elizabeth Plumridge, *Social Research on HIV/AIDS in New Zealand: A Bibliography 1984-1993*, Auckland, 1994.

History

(see also *Regional Bibliographies*)

Guide to New Zealand Information Sources, Part VI: History, compiled by V. J. Hector, Palmerston North, 1982.

There is a substantial bibliography, or rather a series of select bibliographies, in *The Oxford History of New Zealand Second Edition*, edited by Geoffrey W. Rice, Auckland, 1992.

New Zealand historical publications are included in the *Annual Bulletin of Historical Literature*, London, 1911–.

Immigration and ethnic relations

Paul Spoonley et al., *Immigration and Immigrants: a New Zealand Bibliography*, 2nd ed., revised by H. M. McIntyre, Wellington, 1985.

Andrew D. Trlin and Paul Spoonley, *New Zealand and International Migration: A Digest and Bibliography*, 2 vols, Palmerston North, 1986, 1992.

Barbara Thomson, *Ethnic Groups in New Zealand: a bibliography*, Wellington, 1993.

There is a bibliography in Paul Spoonley, David Pearson and Cluny Macpherson, ed., *Nga Patai: racism and ethnic relations in Aotearoa/New Zealand*, Palmerston North, 1996.

Labour and industrial relations

H. O. Roth, *New Zealand Trade Unions: A Bibliography*, 2nd ed., Auckland, 1977, a revised and retitled continuation of his *Labour Legislation in New Zealand: A Bibliography*, Auckland, 1964.

P. Brosnan, *New Zealand Labour and Employment Research, 1859-1990: a bibliography of research and research materials*, Wellington, c1991.

Since 1987 the Trade Union History Project, based in Wellington, has promoted research and publications.

There is a comprehensive bibliography in John E. Martin, *Holding the Balance: a history of New Zealand's Department of Labour, 1891-1995*, Wellington, 1996.

Law

For law practitioners is the LINX database [www.linx.org.nz], providing entrance to New Zealand case law, journal articles and textbooks since 1986.

Also on the Internet [www.kennett.co.nz/maorilaw/] is Maori Law Review, a law reporter concentrating on current issues

J. F. Northey, *Index to New Zealand Legal Writing* [1954-1981], 2nd ed., Auckland, Legal Research Foundation, 1982 (includes such subjects as 'armed services', 'local government', and 'Maori land'). This is supplemented by *Index to New Zealand Legal Writing and Cases*, second volume [1982-1985], ed. K. A. Palmer, Auckland, Legal Research Foundation, 1987, and updated by the annual *Current Australian and New Zealand Legal Literature Index*.

Sweet and Maxwell Ltd., *A Legal Bibliography of the British Commonwealth of Nations: Vol. 6, Australia, New Zealand and their Dependencies from Earliest Times to June 1958*, 2nd ed., London, 1958.

Current Australian and New Zealand Legal Literature Index, Sydney, 1973–.

Maori Studies and Race Relations see *Finding Maori Information: 10.4*

Military

H. O. Roth, *Pacifism in New Zealand: A Bibliography*, Auckland, 1966.

C. E. Dornbusch, compiler, *The New Zealand Army: a bibliography*, Cornwallville, New York, 1961.

Penelope Wheeler, compiler, *New Zealand Bibliography of World War Two*, Wellington, 1977.

There have been published 'official' — or government-supported — accounts of New Zealand's several wars: James Cowan's *The New Zealand Wars: A History of the Maori Campaigns and the Pioneering Period* (1922), for example, or the *Official History of New Zealand in the Second World War 1939-45* in over 40 volumes. Recent example is the two volume *New Zealand and the Korean War*, by Ian McGibbon, Auckland 1992 and 1996.

Natural history

Guide to New Zealand Information Sources, Parts I, IIA, IIB, [cf. above **4.1**] compiled by Lucy E. Battye, N. Thompson, and Craig Cherrie respectively, Palmerston North, 1975, 1977.

Politics

There is a ten and a half page bibliography in Richard Mulgan, *Politics in New Zealand*, 2nd ed., Auckland, 1997; detailed (Labour Party) bibliographies in Keith Sinclair, *Walter Nash*, Auckland, 1976, and Erik Olssen, *John A. Lee*, Dunedin, 1977; and a bibliography in Barry Gustafson, *The First 50 Years: A History of the New Zealand National Party*, Auckland, 1986.

N. E. Archer and Mary Langton, compilers, *Tweedledum and Tweedledee, General Elections in New Zealand: A Bibliography Including some By-Elections*, Wellington, 1975. (This is more useful than the title might suggest.)

M. D. Coleman, *New Zealand Labour Party 1916-1966: A Bibliography*, Wellington, 1972.

Regional studies

G. J. Griffiths, *Books of Southern New Zealand*, Dunedin, 1989.

Bibliography of the Waikato Region, ed. R. C. Hallett and A. P. U. Millett, Hamilton, 1988.

Robert de Zouche Hall, *Gisborne and the East Coast: Local History Sources: An Introduction*, 2nd ed., revised and enlarged, Gisborne, 1984.

Kathryn Rountree, *An Historical and Archaeological Bibliography of the Bay of Islands*, Auckland, 1984.

Mervyn Austin Nixon, *A Bibliography of the Manawatu*, Palmerston North, 1979, with a *Supplement* by Christopher Campbell for the years 1978-1982.

Religion

Peter J. Lineham and Anthony R. Grigg, *Religious History of New Zealand: a bibliography*, 4th ed., Palmerston North, 1993.

Guide to New Zealand Information Sources, Part IV: Religion, compiled by L. E. Marsden, Palmerston North, 1980.

(Note, too, Coralie Jenkin, compiler, *Collections of Religion and Theology in Australia and New Zealand,* Adelaide, 1992.)

Science

see above **4.11** (note New Zealand Science)

B. N. Thompson and Bruce W. Hayward, *Bibliography of New Zealand Earth Sciences Excursion Guides 1891-1990*, Lower Hutt, 1991.

Note, also, Bruce W. Hayward, David Shelley and Bruce N. Thompson, ed., *Bibliography of New Zealand earth science theses (up to December 1987)*, Lower Hutt, 1989;
Bibliography of New Zealand Antarctic [Research] Programme Publications, 3 vols, Christchurch, 1975, 1985, 1994;
Division of Marine and Freshwater Science: list of publications 1954-1986, compiled by R. M. C. Thompson, Wellington 1987;
A. T. Hoban and J. Kenny, *Mineral Bibliography of New Zealand, 1990*, 1990 — compiled from the Minlit bibliographic database;
A Bibliography of Scientific Papers, Theses, Conference Papers and Reports from Work undertaken in the National Climate Laboratory, 1972-1994, [edited by E. A. Halligan], Palmerston North, 1995.

Campbell S. Nelson and Wilma M. Blom, *Publication Record for the Department of Earth Sciences, University of Waikato: the first twenty-one years (1970-1990)*, Hamilton, 1992.

Patricia Walbridge, *Technological change and New Zealand society : a bibliography* [photocopied], Wellington, 1986.

G. M. Reid, A. G. Matheson, G. M. Walton, *Bibliography of New Zealand Apiculture, 1842-1986*, Tauranga, 1988.

Sexuality and gender studies

A. P. U. Millett, *Bibliography on Homosexuality in New Zealand*, Hamilton, 1995.

Linda Hill and Charles Crothers, *The Literature on New Zealand Sexuality: a selectively annotated bibliography*, Auckland, 1988 [for period from the 1970s]

There are bibliographies in Bev James and Kay Saville-Smith, *Gender, Culture and Power: challenging New Zealand's gendered culture*, 2nd ed., Auckland 1994; Jock Phillips, *A Man's Country: the Image of the Pakeha Male, a history*, rev. ed., Auckland, 1996; and — also dealing with Pakeha — Claire Toynbee, *Her Work and His; family, kin and community in New Zealand 1900-1930*, Wellington, 1995.

Social Science

Finding Social Science Research: an information directory, compiled by Dallas and Vasantha Krishnan, Wellington, 1994.

Patricia Walbridge, *Technological change and New Zealand society: a bibliography* [photocopied], Wellington, 1986.

Sport and Recreation

Bronwyn Rickerby and Jeanette King, *Leisure and Recreation in New Zealand: a research register (1974-1991)* (Lincoln University Department of Parks, Recreation and Tourism, Occasional Paper no. 7), 1992.

Diana S. Neave, *Recreation Studies in New Zealand: a bibliography*, Wellington, 1977.

Hillary Commission for Recreation and Sport, *Diploma for Recreation and Sport: library list of all final projects*, Wellington, 1989.

Clare Simpson, *Women and Recreation in Aotearoa/New Zealand: an annotated bibliography*, [1991].

Statistics

Statistics New Zealand, *Catalogue,* Wellington, 1994– (replaces catalogues issued under different titles since 1962).

New Zealand. Department of Statistics, *Statistical Publications, 1840-1960,* Wellington, 1961 (— more widely held and easier to find than a later update: *Statistical Publications, 1840-1980,* the separate chapters of which were published in 1981 in successive issues of the then Department's circular, *Advice to Libraries).*[Note also **Reference Works: 4.12** Statistics.]

R. P. Hargreaves and L. D. B. Heenan, *An Annotated Bibliography of New Zealand Population,* Dunedin, 1972.

Cyril Mako, *A Directory of the location of statistics on the New Zealand Maori population from official sources: Putunga Tatautanga Maori,* Wellington, 1991. [See too **Finding Maori Information: 10.4.3**.]

The Health Information Service of the Ministry of Health, formerly National Health Statistics Centre, Department of Health (cf. their *Publications Index,* 1986), collects, collates and publishes health statistics. Databases are available on the Internet.

Tourism

Tourism Research Bibliography, 1985-mid 1994, Wellington, 1995.

Women's studies

(and see also above, *Family*)

Patricia Ann Sargison, *Victoria's Furthest Daughters: a bibliography of Published Sources for the Study of Women in New Zealand, 1830-1914,* Wellington, 1984.

Neil Heinz, *Women in New Zealand; A List of Material Issued 1950-1978,* Auckland, 1980.

Bibliography of SROW publications, 1966-1983, Wellington, 1984 [SROW = Society for Research on Women in New Zealand].

Rosemary Seymour, compiler, *Women's Studies in New Zealand 1974-1977: A Pilot Bibliography-Directory*, Hamilton, 1978, with *Supplements* to 1979.

There is an annotated bibliography by Anishka Jelicich in Claudia Scott ed., *Women and Taxation*, Wellington, 1993.

Note also Susan F. Bailey's *Women and the British Empire: An Annotated Guide to Sources,* New York and London, 1983, and the City of London Polytechnic's microfiche catalogue, *Biblio Fem* [cited above, **5.2**].

6. Periodicals and Newspapers

6.1 Periodicals
6.2 Newspapers

6.1 Periodicals

Articles on New Zealand are found scattered in a host of likely and unlikely places: all major branches of traditional study have generated their own specialist journals and these will be found in university libraries. But financial stringencies limit the extent to which libraries can keep up subscriptions to overseas publications and serious research work, even though focused on New Zealand, requires checking out the periodicals material produced overseas. The only way to do that is to search the appropriate subject abstracts and/or the broadly encompassing periodicals indexes.

For searching New Zealand periodicals — or even minor and ephemeral material — browsing is pleasurable and rewarding. But it is haphazard and even here it is best to follow the more systematic approach of going directly to

• *Index New Zealand*, 1987–, CD-ROM, online as INNZ.

Successor to the old printed *Index to New Zealand Periodicals*, Wellington, 1941-86, *Index New Zealand* contains a comprehensive index to articles in New Zealand scholarly journals which are half a page or more long, together with a selective index to articles from overseas journals and general interest New Zealand journals. The *Index* is divided into distinct sequences of entries: 'General', 'Author', 'Book Reviews', and 'Corporate and Personal Names'. There are cumulative issues of the fiche through the year.

For the student of 'early' New Zealand, there is H. E. M. Fildes, *Selective Indexes* [above **4.7**: Biography]. There is also a 26-page tightly packed list of New Zealand periodical articles, arranged by subject, in *Combined Retrospective Index Set to Journals in History 1838-1974*, ed. Annadel N. Wile et al., vol. 4, Washington, 1977, pp. 164-89.

Periodical business and trade literature is indexed in the monthly *Newzindex*, 1979–, which is available on the Internet [**2.2**] via Knowledge Basket [www.knowledge-basket.co.nz].

To find holdings of more obscure journals and to uncover periodicals relevant to a specialised field of research, reference might be made to the National Library's Te Puna [**2.2**]. Until 1995 an annual microfiche, *The Finding List*, replaced and updated the printed *Union*

List of Serials in New Zealand Libraries, 3rd ed., Wellington, 1970, and *Supplement 1970-1975*, but gave less bibliographic information (the minimum in fact).

Of course there is a wealth of periodical indexes, available in print and on CD-ROM and the Internet, as each country develops its own research tools. For example, the Australians have *Australian Public Affairs Information Service: Subject Index to Current Literature*, [APAIS] Canberra, 1945–.

Two leading international indexes to periodicals are:

• *Social Sciences Index* (which succeeds *International Index* and the later, first *Social Sciences and Humanities Index*, and then *Humanities Index*, 1916-74)

• *British Humanities Index*, London, 1962–

The latter is one of the successors to *The Subject Index to Periodicals*; the other successor is *The British Technology Index*. Both indexes are available on CD-ROM, the *British Humanities Index* with the title *BHI plus*.

Of appeal to the browser is the little weekly, *Current Contents Arts & Humanities*, Philadelphia, 1979– , now online, which reproduces journals' contents tables, along with author and title word indexes, and three-monthly cumulative indexes.

Very useful sometimes are the summaries of articles given in various abstracts: *Geographical Abstracts, Abstracts of English Studies*, and so forth. These compilations can be very substantial in their coverage: *Historical Abstracts* publishes more than 8000 citations a year from 2000 journals in some ninety countries. Most of this material is on CD-ROM and/or online. On CD-ROM, for example, as INSPEC, are the several series into which *Science Abstracts* has split, the British *ASSIA plus MS-DOS ed* (*Applied Social Sciences Index & Abstracts Plus*) and the American *PAIS International*.

Through a library there is access to a variety of databases on the Internet, bibliographic and full text. Some bibliographic systems provide a document supply service.

Various publications of course produce their own indexes, though these can be erratic and often not easy to find. With scholarly serials of small circulation, albeit high reputation, the appearance of an occasional index depends on editorial whim, and cumulative indexes are even less likely to appear. Significant exceptions are the Turnbull Library's *Index to the New Zealand Listener 1939-1987*, on microfiche, Wellington, 1995, and indexes to *Notornis* and to the *Journal of Agriculture*: *Fifty Years of Bird Study in New Zealand: an index to Notornis, 1939-1989*, by B. D. Heather and P. M Sheehan, Wellington, 1990, and *New Zealand Journal of Agriculture*, *consolidated general index*, 1946– (covering volumes 1 to 110, 1910-1965).

Also most valuable for some researchers are indexes compiled for publications long since deceased like *Tomorrow* (J. J. Herd compiler, *Index to Tomorrow 1934-40*, Dunedin, 1962) or *Woman Today*, Wellington, 1937-39 (a monthly magazine written by women concerned with 'peace, freedom and progress'; republished by the Turnbull Library in 1990 on microfiche).

6.2 Newspapers

The great unofficial printed source material is the newspaper and, more recently, the periodical and trade and house journal. News pages and — even more perhaps — advertisements provide material for studies of all facets of daily life. A useful little brochure is the Alexander Turnbull Library's, *New Zealand Newspapers: How to Use Them for Research*, Wellington, 1989. A steady stream of comment and a wealth of social history is found, too, in the great number of magazines and journals which have waxed and waned over the decades. Some newspapers now can be accessed electronically on the Internet, such as *The Press*, Christchurch, *The Dominion*, Wellington, and other publications of Independent Newspapers Ltd (part-owned by the media magnate Rupert Murdoch) which can be accessed on the INLN database. The business weeklies *The Independent* and *National Business Review* are available electronically.

The *List of Newspapers and Magazines Placed on the Register at the Post Office Headquarters, Wellington*, Wellington, 1886-1986, for a hundred years gave an almost complete list of newspapers and magazines published in New Zealand. For a useful account of the development of major newspapers, there is G. H. Scholefield's *Newspapers in New Zealand*, Wellington, 1958 (although it is marred by errors and omissions). There is an article on the circulation figures of some late nineteenth-century newspapers in *Archifacts* for April 1988/January 1989.

The main New Zealand repositories for newspapers are the Turnbull and Parliamentary Libraries, especially for newspapers published since the passage of the 1903 Copyright Act. The guide to holdings of newspapers is D. R. Harvey's *Union List of Newspapers Preserved in Libraries, Newspaper Offices, Local Authority Offices and Museums in New Zealand*, Wellington, 1987 — an indispensable aid for anyone who wishes to consult earlier and less accessible newspapers. For these the main repositories are the Hocken and Turnbull Libraries (and also, incidentally, the British Library in London, although, considering the masses of early newspapers forwarded to England, this last collection is disappointing). Significant change to the Turnbull Library's holdings since Harvey's *Union List* was published has been transference to the Turnbull of a number of old newspapers and periodicals previously held in the Parliamentary and main National Library collections. It is worth noting, too, that various libraries now have microfilm copies of important runs of newspapers, some of which can be obtained by purchase or through interloan: see especially the results of over twenty years of a microfilming programme at the National Library: *New Zealand Newspapers on Microfilm*, Wellington, 1995, which lists titles available from the Library.

Guide to Niupepa, 1842-1933 Maori newspapers, Wellington, 1996, microfiche, is arranged chronologically by title listing periodicals (Niupepa) published in Maori or for Maori readers. In the years 1842-1933 there were three types published: government-sponsored, iwi-based, and religious, though by the twentieth century they were mostly religious.

Newzindex (commercial and technical articles) and *Index New Zealand* [above **6.1**] selectively index some newspapers as well as periodicals: *Index New Zealand* indexes the main centre dailies and Sunday papers and some Maori newspapers. In addition, as well as the newspapers themselves some libraries — notably the Parliamentary Library — over the years maintained card indexes to their collections of newspapers while nowadays they can retrieve items electronically. The public libraries in the main centres have indexes to their local newspapers. As well, there is the NINX database [see **2.2**: the Knowledge Basket].

The Alexander Turnbull Library has on microfiche an *Index to Early Wellington Newspapers 1839-1865*, 1995, and *Index to the New Zealand Mail 1871-1907*, 1995. Libraries compile in-house lists and finding aids: the Alexander Turnbull Library, for example, has a regional guide to Wellington newspapers (1995). One newspaper, the *Northern Advocate*, has a printed index for a few years (1946-58). But indexes are not available for many early New Zealand newspapers; for anyone wishing to follow up issues of the past it is usually necessary to plough through a paper, issue by issue.

Kathryn Peacocke, *Newspaper Indexes in New Zealand: Guide*, Hamilton, 1994, is intended to collate sources which are not available through national networks, although it does also include newspapers indexed by the Alexander Turnbull Library for the 'Names' index of INNZ (*Index New Zealand*). Previously, a provisional list of indexes along with collections of clippings was given in the 1986 edition of A. P. U. Millett and F. T. H. Cole, *Bibliographical Work in New Zealand. Union List of Newspapers.* D. R. Harvey's *Union List of Newspapers* also notes indexes.

Over the years a local library may have accumulated, or been given by research enthusiasts, a significant horde of cuttings and materials. As may other research institutes. A major politics collection, for example, has been built up since the 1960s at the University of Auckland Political Studies Department. From 1989 Newsline Services

Ltd, Auckland, cut and filed all the articles from the main daily newspapers and national magazines (see *Newsline Information Library Catalogue*). It also produces a *Newsline: Fortnightly Digest of New Zealand News*, Auckland, 1989–, with cumulative indexes as *Newsline: Current Archives of New Zealand News*, 1991–.

Cuttings relating to New Zealand from *The Times*, London, have been compiled by that paper's Intelligence Department and published by University Microfilms, in three volumes, 1927-59. There are available indexes, printed or on microfilm, to *The Times* from 1906, and to the *New York Times* from 1913. The electronic edition of the *Official Index to The Times, 1906–1980* available on the Internet and CD-ROM contains twelve million articles, charting the course of much of the twentieth century. The previously issued *Palmer's Index to The Times*, on CD-ROM in 1994, also made available online, takes the coverage to almost 200 years of British, British imperial and world history. Other major newspapers also, of course, are accessible online and/or on CD-ROM.

7. Official Documents and Records

Building studies around governmental sources may, indeed normally does, lead to an excessive state-orientation and yet in many ways is inescapable. Directly, or indirectly, so much of the story of the New Zealand society derives from official sources. The state is the greatest distributor of largesse, the principal sponsor of research — for example, in addition to research sponsored through educational institutions, since the late 1990s government's Marsden Fund, named after the scientist Sir Ernest Marsden, and administered by the Royal Society, has been expanded and its range broadened to include pure research or 'blue skies' research in the humanities as well as in science. (The Marsden Fund supports curiosity-driven research; the far larger Public Good Science Fund supports applied research.) Through its agencies, inquiries, policy proposals and policy implementation, the state is the generator of discussion, and — frequently — the significant decision-maker. The 'Crown' figures at the highest level of formal decision-taking; but throughout the public sector are the policy makers and fact-gatherers.

The major published official sources may be categorised as:

- Central government publications and records
- Parliamentary publications, consisting of parliamentary proceedings (debates and journals) and appended papers
- Statutes, regulations and law reports
- Local and regional government publications and records

- Publications and records of other countries, historically British records in particular, and of international agencies and organisations — for example, the United Nations, the World Bank and International Monetary Fund, ILO (International Labour Organisation), OECD (Organisation for Economic Co-operation and Development).

For the last-mentioned category see *International Bibliography: Publications of Intergovernmental Organisations*, New York, 1983–, a continuation of *International Bibliography, Information, Documentation*, 1973–. There is also *UNDOC: Current Index: United Nations Documents Index*, 1979–, covering all United Nations material. Different agencies, too, may publish United Nations material on CD-ROM: the *Earth Summit*, the complete record of the 1992 United Nations Conference on Environment and Development, has been published as a cooperative venture between Canada's International Development Research Centre, the United Nations and the Canadian Centre for Health and Safety — on one disk the equivalent of over 50,000 printed pages.

The New Zealand Law Commission has produced a basic guide to international law as it affects New Zealand law, which includes information on the sources of international law, and even a handy glossary of the acronyms of which international bodies and commentators are so fond: *A New Zealand Guide to International Law and its Sources*, 1996.

With its exchange arrangements, and its responsibility for holding New Zealand official material, the Parliamentary Library has always been the most important repository for official publications. Overseas material is held in the Library's Documents Collection, to which (unlike the rest of the Library) members of the general public have access as of right.

J. B. Ringer, *An Introduction to New Zealand Government*, Christchurch, 1991 [above, **4.10**], is an indispensable aid to anyone needing to explore New Zealand's official documents and records. Also already noted are: booklet by C. L. Carpenter, 1994, Part V of the *Guide to New Zealand Information Sources*, and *New Zealand Government Directory*.

The unofficial, but invaluable record of government decisions, proposals and regulations, is the little weekly newsletter

- *The Capital Letter: a weekly review of administration, legislation & law*, 1978–

not the less invaluable for its comprehensive cumulative indexes issued at intervals through the year [searchable, under the heading 'The Law', at www.nbr.co.nz].

7.1 Central government

7.1.1 Government departments and agencies

Much central government material, even if also available as separate publications, printed or electronic, is included in the annual parliamentary papers: the multi-volume *Appendices to the Journals of the House of Representatives* [below, **7.1.2**]. But there are also the data services of many government departments of state and quasi-autonomous agencies, as well as a variety of publications. The Ministry of Justice, for example, generates a number of reports and discussion papers which can be downloaded from its home page. The Ministry of Foreign Affairs and Trade produces information booklets and its *New Zealand Foreign Affairs and Trade Record* (with various name changes over the years, reflecting its publisher's name changes), 1950–, and, as previously noted [**4.4**], the Reserve Bank of New Zealand its *Bulletin*, 1938–. The *New Zealand Official Yearbook*, 1893–, provides valuable distillation from the output of Statistics New Zealand, but for the range of present and past published material see its *Catalogue*, and *Statistical Publications, 1840-1960* [cited above, **5.3.1**: Statistics].

Following passage of freedom of information legislation, there was available a *Directory of Official Information* 1983–, originally published by the State Services Commission, (editions of 1983, 1985), now, since 1989, by the Official Information Unit, Ministry of Justice, Wellington. New editions have been brought out every few years. Fully indexed, with cross references, the book describes the structures and functions of state departments and agencies, with a general description of the documents they hold and of how to obtain access to information, including whom to contact for inquiries. Of course access to the most up-to-date information is through the Internet: New Zealand Government Online [already cited above **4.10**]. (For an account of the development of the state services, see R. J. Polaschek's *Government Administration in New Zealand*, Wellington, 1958, and *Reshaping the State: New Zealand's Bureaucratic Revolution*, ed. Jonathan Boston et al., Auckland, 1991.)

The official voice of government has always been *The New Zealand Gazette*, 1841–, a dry, poorly indexed publication of limited value, which nonetheless contains official notices covering the whole compass of executive acts — including the dramatic and the colourful: war, accession of a new monarch, sacking of a minister. For a time, 1848-53, the *Gazette* was issued separately for the two provinces of New Ulster and New Munster. In practice, government largely speaks direct to the news media. Through the Internet it is possible to get direct access to major political speeches and party policies. For a time there were issued *Press Statements by Ministers of the Crown*, Wellington, 1955-73.

It should be remembered that official publications are an expression of bureaucratic order and organisation and no bureaucracy is perfect: there are sometimes surprising instances of official absent-mindedness. As one moves back in time, too, the pakeha orientation of governmental activity, and hence of official documentation, becomes ever more apparent.

There have been published official or quasi-official histories of some major state services — such as John E. Martin, *Holding the Balance: a history of the Department of Labour, 1891-1995*, Wellington, 1995 [mentioned above **5.3.1**: 'Labour'], or Bronwyn Dalley, *Family Matters: Child Welfare in Twentieth-century New Zealand*, 1998. The Internal Affairs Department in particular has been important in providing a home for various historical endeavours: the studies of the National Historical Committee (set up in 1936 for the 1940 centennial); publications of the War History Branch of the department (established 1945) on the second world war [see **5.3.1**: Military and **9.2**: Published collections of selected documents]; the various useful post-war works emanating from the (renamed, 1963) Historical Publications Branch (including the *New Zealand Atlas* [cited **4.5**]); and collections of documents on post-war external relations. Most recently the Department has hosted the Dictionary of New Zealand Biography unit.

7.1.2 Parliamentary publications

A useful pamphlet is the *Users' Guide to Parliamentary Publications*, prepared in the office of the Clerk of the House of Representatives, Wellington, 1989. The chapter on 'Parliamentary Publications' in J. B. Ringer's *An Introduction to New Zealand Government* is a full and detailed account. The article by J. O. Wilson, 'The papers of parliament', *New Zealand Libraries* 25 (1962): 213-24, is still of historical interest.

Proceedings and debates

Under a British act of 1852 New Zealand's parliament — formally, until 1986, a 'General Assembly' — comprised an elected House of Representatives, an appointed Legislative Council and the Governor (Governor-General from 1917). The Legislative Council was abolished effective 1 January 1951, leaving a single-chamber parliament. Today the term 'New Zealand Parliament' customarily is used to refer to the House of Representatives alone, although under the 1986 Constitution Act the New Zealand parliament comprises the House of Representatives along with the Sovereign or the Governor-General as the Sovereign's representative.

The main record of Parliament's proceedings is the *New Zealand Parliamentary Debates*, 1867–, commonly known as *Hansard* after its British parent. Eventually available in bound volumes, initially *Hansard* is issued seriatim in paperback with pink covers as 'Hansard pinks' — latterly there have also been separate green paperbacks containing written answers to questions MPs have submitted to ministers, giving a mass of miscellaneous and detailed information. There are volumes of the *Debates* for the years 1854 to 1866, but these were compiled years later from newspaper reports and other sources; although useful, and normally quoted as though reliable, they are incomplete and it is impossible to determine just how accurate they are. Even the later debates reports are not entirely accurate since they are subject to some tidying up, and revision by Members of Parliament. The parliamentary debates and parliamentary questions are also available through the Internet. In recent years the Office of the Clerk of the House of Representatives has compiled the *Parliamentary Bulletin*, 1986–, a running account of parliament's business in hand. More useful in the longer term is another work emanating from the Clerk's Office: *Notes on Parliamentary Law and Procedure*, 1989–, a review of significant developments in parliament. (As already mentioned above, **4.4**, brief summaries also are found in the publication of the Commonwealth Parliamentary Association, *The Parliamentarian*. *The Table*, too, as the journal of clerks-at-the-table in Commonwealth parliaments records what they deem to be significant.)

The *Votes and Proceedings*, 1854-6, and *Journals*, 1858–, of the New Zealand House of Representatives merely record parliament's formal proceedings and are of limited value, though they do include some material not elsewhere recorded, for example schedules and tables, and a few committee reports, and they may also be used to supplement the *New Zealand Parliamentary Debates* up to 1867. Today the *Journals*, like the *Debates* (*Hansard*) and *Appendices* to the *Journals* [below: Parliamentary papers], appear in paperback segments eventually accumulated in bound volumes. A *General Index to the Journals* ... has been published in four volumes, covering the years 1854-92, 1893-1902, 1903-17, and 1918-23. The *Journals of the Legislative Council* were published separately from the *Journals* of the lower house.

The procedural rules under which the present-day parliament operates are easily found: David McGee's *Parliamentary Practice in New Zealand*, 2nd ed., Wellington, 1994, is an excellent work now in need of some revision but libraries should have the latest, post-1995, edition of the *Standing Orders of the House of Representatives*. Past rules, however, are not so easily found, especially for the early years of the parliament. After 1854, the major revisions have been 1856, 1894, 1925, 1929, 1951, 1962, and then a succession of revisions at about five-year intervals. Major changes, including the renumbering of the Orders, occurred in 1985. In 1995, following approval by referendum in 1993 of the MMP (proportional representation voting) system, parliament underwent the most extensive overhaul of its standing orders since the first drafts were prepared in the 1850s. (For summary of the changes — as well as for description of the MMP electoral system — see *New Zealand Under MMP*, by Jonathan Boston et al., Auckland, 1996: Table 5.1 shows procedure changes.) For changes in recent decades, and their rationale, see the preceding reports of the parliamentary committees which reviewed the Orders, found in the *Appendices to the Journals of the House of Representatives.*

How the chair interprets the Standing Orders depends in part on the decisions of successive speakers — see *Speakers' Rulings 1867 to 1989 Inclusive*, Wellington, 1990 — and in part on the guidance given by 'Erskine May', the renowned Sir T. Erskine May, *Treatise on the Law, Privileges, Proceedings and Usages of Parliament*, first published in 1844 and now in its twenty-first edition: *Erskine May's Treatise ...*, ed. C. J. Boulton, London, 1989. Most libraries will not have copies of old editions of either May or the New Zealand *Standing Orders.*

The proceedings of parliament's predecessor, the old, appointed Legislative Council of New Zealand, 1841 to 1853, are available in contemporary newspapers, and also in the *New Zealand Government Gazette*, except for Sessions I to VI and XII, which were issued separately. The Parliamentary Library holds two bound volumes, *Minutes of the Legislative Council of New Zealand 1841-1844* and *Minutes of the Legislative Council of New Zealand 1845-1853; New Munster 1848-1849*, which include extracts from the *Gazettes*.

Parliamentary papers

For the first parliamentary sessions of 1854, 1855, and 1856, journals and appended papers appeared together in *Votes and Proceedings of the House of Representatives*. Since then parliamentary papers have been published separately as *Appendices to the Journals of the House of Representatives*. (They are usually referred to in the plural, although each individual volume is entitled *Appendix ...* and so catalogued.) Here are found the annual reports of government departments, agencies, and commissions, many of the reports of committees of the House (although some exist only in manuscript), and other papers and documents presented to Parliament by the Government. The latter include exchanges with foreign governments and international organisations, financial statements, background papers, and more — the *Appendices* are a mine of information, and much more conveniently and rationally organised than, for example, the British or Australian parliamentary papers. Papers are given 'shoulder numbers' — such as A. 9, B. 6 — in which the letter stands for a broad subject category or class, and the number for a particular paper. The letter categories are currently:

[A] Legislative and Foreign Affairs
[B] Finance, Revenue, etc.
[C] Land, Agriculture and Environment
[D] Resources and Energy

[E] Welfare and Justice
[F] Communications
[G] General
[H] Commissions, Royal Commissions
[I] Reports and Proceedings of Select Committees.

Papers are given the same shoulder-numbers each year: thus, the Budget appears each year as B. 6. The last major rationalisation of the subject categories was effected in 1973: J. O. Wilson, 'New Zealand parliamentary papers: changes in shoulder numbers', *New Zealand Libraries* 37 (1974): 131-5, describes and lists the resulting changes.

Since 1934 the bound volumes of the *Appendices to the Journals of the House of Representatives* normally have included sessional indexes. As well, consolidated indexes have been published for 1854-1913 (1915), 1914-22 (1924), 1923-38 (1952), 1939-53 (1958), and 1954-63 (1965). The first indexes included references also to the Legislative Council papers, but these were of far less value, and of very little value indeed in the decades before the Council was abolished in 1950. Even when at its most active, the upper house only published papers if they were not included in the lower house's *Appendices*. The *Appendices to the Journals of the Legislative Council* are cited as a separate series, but have usually been bound together with the Council's *Journals*.

7.1.3 Laws and regulations

On laws and regulations — as on the whole range of official publications — full coverage is given in J. B. Ringer's *A n Introduction to New Zealand Government*, chapter 13, and, as also noted above, *Capital Letter* seeks to record all significant legislation.

The LINX database and Knowledge Basket were noted above, [2.2], and [5.3: law]; generally, it may be said that provision of information electronically is at least as developed in the field of law as in any other major subject area. While much is fairly readily found via the Knowledge Basket, or for example, the Auckland District Law Society's site [www.adls.org.nz] — which conveniently provides links to New Zealand's top legal sites — to appreciate the scope of information now accessible it is necessary to consult specialist law librarians. For most legal information obtained electronically there is a **charge to be paid**.

Statutes

In addition to their being available online and their inclusion today in legal databases on the Internet [2.2], drafts of bills presented to parliament, and proposed amendments, are printed and copies are available in libraries. Enacted laws are published individually and also in annual bound volumes, the *Statutes of New Zealand*.

Major consolidated or reprinted editions of statutes are:

Consolidated Statutes of the Dominion of New Zealand, 5 vols, Wellington, 1908

The Public Acts of New Zealand (Reprint) 1908-1931, 9 vols, Wellington, 1932-3

Reprint of the Statutes of New Zealand 1908-1957, 16 vols, Wellington, 1958-61.

Since 1979 there has been a succession of volumes of *Reprinted Statutes of New Zealand*, which incorporate amendments to a statute up to the date of its reprinting. Previously, such reprinted acts were bound with the annual bound volumes. Early New Zealand statutes were in 1871 reprinted, for the years of crown colony government, as *Ordinances of the Legislative Council of New Zealand and of the Legislative Council of the Province of New Munster 1841-1853* and, for the succeeding years, as *Statutes of the General Assembly of New Zealand 1854 to 1860*.

In recent decades, law firms and law libraries have had their collections of statutes annotated annually to show amendments made by parliament. The indispensable aids to anyone interested in the evolution of New Zealand law are *Butterworths Annotations* of the New Zealand statutes. These are designed to be read in conjunction with the bound volumes of statutes, and include tables of amendments to acts and notes on cases: thus they both trace the various changes made to statute law and indicate the interpretations of statute made by the courts. From 1982 they were loose-leaf and updated monthly. Earlier sets include: *Butterworths Annotations of New Zealand Statutes*, 6 vols, 1929-55; *Butterworths Cases Annotations of the New Zealand Statutes: Reprint 1908-1957*, 2 vols, 1960-61; and *Butterworths Annotations of the New Zealand Statutes 1908-1982*, 1982.

Were it necessary to know the law in a particular year, reference might be had to John Curnin's *Index to the Laws of New Zealand*, Wellington, published in twenty-seven editions from 1879 to 1933. In 1862, 1877, 1882, and 1890, the *Appendices to the Journals of the House of Representatives* included official lists of Acts in force, but these lacked subject indexes except to provincial legislation. From 1945 to 1964, and again from 1974 to 1976, the final volume of the annual bound volumes of statutes included tables of Acts in force. Since 1979 there has been a separate volume: *Tables of New Zealand Acts and Ordinances and Statutory Regulations in Force* (for some years, till 1985, *Tables of New Zealand Public Acts ...*).

Statutory regulations

Parliament makes law. In many cases, however, it leaves out significant details, delegating to Government power to fill these in, and in such cases government regulations normally have the same force as if enacted by parliament itself. For decades, decrees, proclamations, orders-in-council, or regulations in other form normally were published in the *New Zealand Gazette*. There is now a separate publication, *Statutory Regulations*,Wellington, 1938–, which covers the period from 1936, the year in which a Regulations Act came into force providing for new forms for promulgating regulations. As with the statutes, *Statutory Regulations* can be kept up to date by annual annotations. [Note Status Publishing Ltd [www.status.co.nz] above **2.2**]

Law reports

Judges, also, make law — and they have brought before them all facets of their contemporary society. The University of Waikato Law Library gives information about New Zealand case law, in print and electronic, at www.waikato.ac.nz/lawlib/index/html.

   The *New Zealand Law Reports* date from 1883 (on the database LEXIS [see **2: 2**] since 1970 and also now via Butterworths [www.butterworths.com.au]). There are available, also, reports of cases prior to 1883, and of Privy Council and District (Magistrates) Courts decisions. As noted above [**5.3** Law] the database LINX for legal personnel provides entrance to case law (namely it gives headnotes to decisions). Texts of decisions of the Privy Council, Court of Appeal, Employment Court, Maori Court and Commerce Commission are available from Status Publishing [www.status.co.nz] [**2.2**]. *Butterworths Resource Management Bulletin*, 1994–, reviews new legislation. *Town and Country Planning Appeals*, from 1992 *New Zealand Resource Management Appeals*, contains decisions on town planning and resource management (also at www.rma.co.nz).

   (For more information, see chapter 16, 'Case Law', in J. B. Ringer's *An Introduction to New Zealand Government*.)

7.2 Regional and local government

7.2.1 Provinces

In 1848 New Zealand was divided into two provinces: New Ulster, centring on Auckland, and New Munster, centring on Wellington. As a consequence, a separate New Munster administration was set up, while the Auckland administration was primarily concerned with New Ulster affairs. Many of the records were duplicated: there were two government gazettes, New Munster Legislative Council proceedings and ordinances as well as New Zealand Legislative Council proceedings and ordinances; and each capital had its separate government departments.

In 1853 the two provinces, and their records, were reunited, under the Auckland administration, and six (eventually nine) provinces were created with elected forms of government: a Superintendent or chief executive, and provincial councils. For the next few years the provinces handled many major governmental functions, notably public works, immigration, education, and the organisation of local services (by boroughs and road boards). With the abolition of the provinces in 1876, many of their functions were assumed by the central government, while purely local functions became the responsibility of the multiplicity of counties and boroughs into which the country was divided. An increasing number of ad hoc authorities also developed, concerned each with one particular service: public transport, fire prevention, harbour control, electric-power supply, pest destruction, and so on.

The post-1853 provinces resembled miniature states more than oversized local authorities and, with a variety of titles, their official publications were produced along similar lines to those of a central government and parliament. They consisted of the same three basic categories:

- Executive notices published in a gazette;
- Votes, proceedings, or journals of the legislature (the single chamber provincial council), together with appended papers, such as reports of committees of inquiry and of provincial government departments;
- Provincial laws. (It has become customary to refer to these as 'Ordinances', a term also applied to laws passed by the nominee Legislative Councils before 1854, reserving the term 'Acts' for laws passed by the New Zealand parliament.)

In some cases proceedings and laws were combined in the same volume. In the case of Taranaki and Marlborough, the proceedings were not published at all (but are available at the National Archives). None of the provinces published official reports of its debates; for these it is necessary to turn to newspaper accounts, in conjunction with the journals of proceedings.

Library holdings of provincial publications are given in the *Union List of Serials* which also details the actual publications produced. (A short list of provincial publications is given in the bibliography of the ancient (1933) *Cambridge History of the British Empire*, Vol. 7, Part 2, *New Zealand*, p. 267.)

7.2.2 Local and regional authorities

The New Zealand Business Who's Who [above **4.8**] lists current local governments and authorities as — since 1966 — has *New Zealand Local Government Yearbook* (before 1973 *New Zealand*

Local Authorities Yearbook). The larger cities of New Zealand can trace their existence back to municipal corporations established during the years of the provinces. Post-provincial counties have disappeared or been merged into cities and districts in a massively restructured local government from 1989. From that date too are the present elected regional councils whose functions include some previously performed by various ad hoc authorities. Some ad hoc bodies were replaced by companies, or appointed enterprises. Local authorities publish annual accounts and plans, perhaps handbooks (cf. entries under the four main centres in the *Union List of Serials*), and a few have commissioned detailed factual chronicles.

Centenaries and jubilees have greatly added to the published material on local history, from the local church or school to the province. Occasionally, too, a commissioned chronicle emerges as first-class history. An example of superior local history, with in-depth analyses of the evolution of the different facets of a region, is A. J. Dreaver's *Horowhenua and its People: A Centennial History*, Levin, 1984.

The main published source of local government history, however, is the newspaper and, that apart, it is necessary to refer to unpublished records. To find where they are held, it is necessary to ask the local authority concerned. Some records are deposited in a library or other local institution. Others are held by the local government itself in properly constituted archives.

Material on local government is included in the annual report of the Internal Affairs Department, for many years H. 22 and latterly G. 7 in the *Appendices to the Journals of the House of Representatives*, and there have also been annual reports of the Local Government Commission, H. 28 and later G. 9 — and for many years of the former Local Authorities Loans Board, B. 17. As noted above [4.4], the Department of Internal Affairs issues *Local Authority Election Statistics* (1967–) which include material on elections held since 1959.

From 1874, under varying titles, Statistics New Zealand or its predecessor published annual statistical reports on local authorities. From 1903 until the early 1930s the *Municipal Handbook of New Zealand*, from 1926 combined with the statistical reports as the *Local Authorities Handbook*, contained detailed material on the New Zealand system of local government. Currently, in the 'Hot off the Press' series, is an annual *Local Authority Statistics, Non-trading Activities*.

Past boundaries are given in the *Atlas of New Zealand Boundaries*, 1986– [above, **4.5**. Note also **5.3.1** 'Subject Bibliographies': Regional].

7.3 Official British publications

For years after 1840 New Zealand was under the formal suzerainty of Great Britain. Amongst the official imperial records, published and unpublished, will be found far more material of New Zealand relevance than that which specifically relates to New Zealand. For those needing to find their way through the published material, there is John E. Pemberton's *The Bibliographical Control of Official Publications*, Oxford and New York, 1982 (although the focus of the book is on the present rather than the past which New Zealanders are more likely to want).

British parliamentary papers

Much of the material published in British parliamentary papers is, of course, of direct New Zealand relevance — dispatches to and from New Zealand, and parliamentary reports and inquiries on New Zealand or on general colonial questions. New Zealand university libraries have a fair number of such parliamentary papers, frequently and incorrectly referred to as 'Great Britain. Parliamentary papers relating to New Zealand.' There is a comprehensive set of British parliamentary papers in the Parliamentary Library, and in the 1970s an extensive and expensive programme of reprinting of nineteenth-century papers by the Irish University Press permitted an expansion of their holdings by such libraries as could afford them. Parliamentary material dating back to the sixteenth century is available also in microform.

A useful introduction to British parliamentary papers is P. and G. Ford, *A Guide to Parliamentary Papers*, 3rd ed., Shannon, 1972. The Fords have also compiled a series of select lists or breviates of British parliamentary papers, covering 1833 to the late twentieth century. For a guide to British papers specifically of New Zealand relevance, see:

M. I. Adam et al., *Guide to the Principal Parliamentary Papers Relating to the Dominions, 1812-1911*, Edinburgh, 1913

Index to British Parliamentary Papers on Australia and New Zealand, 1800-1899, 2 vols, Dublin, 1974

J. O. Wilson, *A Finding List of British Parliamentary Papers Relating to New Zealand 1817-1900*, Wellington, 1960

These are selective guides; there are general alphabetical British indexes from 1801 onwards.

Sometimes New Zealand researchers have had occasion to refer to the British Parliamentary Debates (*Hansard*). The Parliamentary

Library holds a set, and other libraries have the debates up to 1939 in microform. There is a detailed *Guide to the Records of Parliament*, by M. F. Bond, London, 1971.

British parliamentary bills, reports, papers, and debates which relate to New Zealand are listed in the bibliography of the 1933 *The Cambridge History of the British Empire*, vol. 7, Part 2, *New Zealand*, pp. 260-3. The general volumes of this *History* likewise list material of general colonial or imperial relevance.

British and imperial law

British law is important for New Zealand for two reasons. First, when in 1840 New Zealand became a British colony, the law to be enforced by local courts was British law as it stood at that date. Some of those old laws have been retained to this day as part of New Zealand's law.

Secondly, it was not until 1947 that the New Zealand parliament gained full, sovereign independence. Before that date, there were various fields of legislation which it could not touch, and the British parliament could still override acts of the New Zealand parliament. Even though this power had meant little for many years, for decades after 1840 British acts were passed which applied to the empire at large — for example concerning merchant shipping — and were therefore applicable to New Zealand.

The Imperial Laws Application Act, 1988, lists all British laws and regulations in force in New Zealand from 1989. For an indication of British statutes previously in force in New Zealand, see Curnin's *Index to the Laws of New Zealand* and *Butterworths Annotations of New Zealand Statutes* [cited above, **7.1.3**].

8. Theses and Research in Progress

8.1 New Zealand
8.2 Theses written overseas

8.1 New Zealand

Some thesis material comes to light in subsequent articles and books, reputedly gaining in readability in the process. Of those remaining unpublished, the student may expect to find the best cited in specialist works. Unfortunately, theses tend to be built upon theses, as part of a specialist and esoteric body of literature. This is inevitable, for researchers cannot ignore the labours of their predecessors, even if the fruits thereof are not published. Addressed to a specific and limited readership, theses are not usually publishable as they stand. They embody supervised research carried out within conventions of scholarly inquiry with a format appropriate for examination presentation. A rule of thumb may be: if research work is first-class then usually it will surface somewhere. It should stimulate journal articles and reports and be distilled through and cited in books and essays. Occasionally, after long gestation, a thesis has led to a scholarly monograph – such as E. N. Olssen's M.A. thesis of 1965 (*John A. Lee*, Dunedin, 1977) or John Miller's Ph.D. thesis of 1954 (*Early Victorian New Zealand: A Study of Racial Tension and Social Attitudes, 1839-1852*, London, 1958, reprinted Wellington, 1974): rare and outstanding examples of how it is possible to polish, improve, edit and expand a thesis for publication. A more recent example is Rachel Barrowman's *A Popular Vision*: *The Arts and the Left in New Zealand 1930-1950*, Wellington, 1991.

Comprehensive lists of theses, arranged chronologically under broad subject groupings, are given in the *Union List of Theses of the University of New Zealand 1910-1954*,[1] compiled by D. L. Jenkins, Wellington, 1956, with ten *Supplements* compiled by librarians at the University of Otago Library, taking the listing up to 1995. All volumes have author indexes, and subject indexes are given for theses after 1962.

---

1 Until 1962, while teaching was carried out in different University Colleges, today formally entitled Universities, degrees were granted by the University of New Zealand, a non-teaching institution of which the University Colleges were a part.

Completed theses and dissertations were catalogued on the New Zealand Bibliographic Network (1999– Te Puna), and are also indexed in the 'Research' section of *Index New Zealand* [above **6.1**] and traceable online as well as being available on CD-ROM. Universities may publish lists of completed research.

Some university departments have issued lists of research work undertaken there, or perhaps published examples of their best work. Such lists, however, may not be readily obtainable nor may they be particularly convenient to use outside the department involved. Mentioned above [**5.3.1**] was B. W. Hayward et al. ed., *Bibliography of New Zealand Earth Science Theses*, 1989. For historians there has been *Theses on the History of New Zealand*, compiled by Margaret D. Rodger, 4 vols, Palmerston North, 1968-72 (with *Supplement*, 1968-82, compiled by Norah D. Mosen, 1985), which covers history theses and research essays completed in New Zealand, Australia, the United Kingdom and the United States of America, subdivided into biographical studies, political history, social history, and economic, agricultural and industrial history.

Information on current research, begun and completed, in specific subject areas may be found in specialist journals, for example, the *New Zealand Geographer*, the *Newsletter*, 1978– of the Women's Studies Association, the *New Zealand Journal of History* (after 1968, previously in *Historical Studies*, Melbourne).

Theses, either bound or on microfilm or microfiche, normally may be obtained on library interloan, although, as with other unpublished material, they may be subject to special copyright restrictions. Indeed, there may be copyright restrictions on anything anybody has written; in quoting and using published and unpublished material, and in the use of public archives, care should always be taken that permission to quote or to use material has been obtained where required [see **Appendix B** on copyright law]. Some theses written before 1949, since when copies have had to be deposited in a university library, are not now obtainable. It is not worthwhile spending much time looking up and chasing such early theses. Indeed, the titles of theses completed before 1927 are not even all recorded (although over the years additional titles, and locations, have been reported).

8.2 New Zealand studies and theses written overseas

Few theses on strictly New Zealand topics are written overseas. Copies of those that have been written tend to turn up in New Zealand in typescript or some published form. But there is research work on New Zealand being undertaken abroad, and New Zealand will appear in various comparative studies — for example a Ph.D. dissertation comparing voting for third parties in Britain, Canada, New Zealand and South Korea ('Support for Third Parties Under Plurality Rule Electoral Systems', by Won-Taek Kang, London School of Economics and Political Science, 1997). There are centres for New Zealand studies in Edinburgh and at Georgetown University, Washington DC, and theses of New Zealand relevance are most likely to be have been presented in North American and British universities, along with, more obviously, Australian universities. To encourage New Zealand studies in the United Kingdom, in 1987 the New Zealand Studies Committee of the University of Edinburgh launched *BRONZ*, the *British Review of New Zealand Studies*. Scholars in Canada, Australia and New Zealand have formed an Association for Canadian Studies in Australia and New Zealand, ACSANZ, whose journal *Australian-Canadian Studies: A Journal for the Humanities and Social Sciences* 1983–, despite its name, includes New Zealand within its comparative compass (although the focus is primarily on Canada).

There is a *Union List of Higher Degree Theses in Australian University Libraries: Cumulative Edition to 1965*, ed. Enid Wylie, Hobart, University of Tasmania Library, 1967, with irregular supplements to 1973 and thereafter annual (except 1983-84) for a number of years, but like so much reference material now better accessed through online databases. For Great Britain the main guide to recent theses is, now online, a massive catalogue, *Index to Theses Accepted for Higher Degrees in the Universities of Great Britain and Ireland*, London, 1950/51–. The Canadian National Library's *Canadian Theses*, Ottawa, 1960/61–, is produced on microform (1980–). A major source for all recent Canadiana (1972–1997), however, is the National Library of Canada's *Canadiana: The National Bibliography*, available on CD-ROM, and the Library's databases also are available online.

A valuable work is the American *Dissertation Abstracts*, Ann Arbor, Michigan, 1938-1969, indexed biennially, which summarises many North American Ph.D. theses. Since 1970 it has continued, in part, as *Dissertation Abstracts International*.

Theses are searchable online through the Internet; for example *Dissertation Abstracts International* is searchable online and is also available on CD-ROM.

There is a New Zealand section in an annual produced by the Institute of Commonwealth Studies, London, *Theses in Progress in Commonwealth Studies*, 1970–. Mentioned above was Margaret Rodger, *Theses on the History of New Zealand*, with its wide-ranging coverage, and other listings of theses in specific subject areas are, of course, available. In history, for example, the Canadian Historical Association publishes an annual *Register of Dissertations*. Lists of British theses, completed and in progress, are published in *Historical Research for University Degrees in the United Kingdom*, London, 1931/2– (until 1966 published as the 'Theses supplement' of the

Bulletin of the Institute of Historical Research, London). The best way to find the handful of past British theses specifically on New Zealand topics is probably to use P. M. Jacobs, *History Theses 1901-70: Historical Research for Higher Degrees in the Universities of the United Kingdom*, London, 1976.

9. Archives and Manuscripts

9.1 Archives and manuscripts: finding aids

Registers and catalogues

A distinction may be drawn between 'manuscripts', the private papers of individuals, and 'archives', the non-current records of an organisation and distinguished by the formal, corporate character of the creating body. Archives are not necessarily hand- or type-written, but may well be printed. In both cases, however, the principal finding aids are the

- *National Register of Archives and Manuscripts in New Zealand*, compiled and edited at the Alexander Turnbull Library, Wellington, 1979–93,

and its predecessor, the

- *Union Catalogue of New Zealand and Pacific Manuscripts in New Zealand Libraries*, interim edition, Wellington, 1968-69.

The old *Union Catalogue* listed library holdings alphabetically, according to the names of the different collections, but it is very incomplete, and it is not indexed or arranged chronologically. The *National Register* aimed to include all significant New Zealand archives and manuscripts — except (since 1983) public archives held by National Archives — and 'to provide an entry for the researcher into the list by time, geographical area or by subject'. The *National Register*, however, was unable to provide a comprehensive guide to manuscript and archive holdings because many institutions were not able to complete and submit up-to-date lists. The development of a database is to be expected. New acquisitions are selectively reported in the archivists' journal, *Archifacts* (which is a mine of information about the past), and the Turnbull's acquisitions are reported very fully in the *Turnbull Library Record*. For older library acquisitions (papers held for more than fifty years), there is the section on manuscripts in the bibliography of *The Cambridge History of the British Empire*, Vol. 7, Part 2, *New Zealand*, ed. J. Holland Rose, A. P. Newton, and E. A. Benians, Cambridge, 1933, pp. 263-7.

As a special suffrage centennial-year edition of the *National Register*, the Turnbull Library published *Archives of Women's Organisations: a register of collections held at New Zealand archives institutions, libraries, museums and historical societies*, Wellington, 1993. (There is a *Directory of Women's Organisations and Groups in New Zealand*, produced by the Ministry of Women's Affairs, Wellington, 1994.) Also published is Alexander Turnbull Library, *Women's Words: A Guide to Manuscripts and Archives in the Alexander Turnbull Library Relating to Women in the Nineteenth Century*, compiled by Diana Meads, Philip Rainer and Kay Sanderson, Wellington, 1988. Sue Loughlin and Carolyn Morris have produced *Womanscripts: a guide to manuscripts in the Auckland Institute and Museum Library relating to Women*, Auckland, 1995, and Wendy Yee, *Women: a subject index to the Canterbury Museum archives and manuscripts collection, 1850-1993*, Christchurch, 1993.

Libraries' finding aids

To help the user of a particular collection of papers, for large archive groups and manuscript collections at least, libraries attempt to compile finding aids: the **series list**, the **inventory**, and the **calendar**.

The **series lists** give the different forms of record to be found in a collection — minutes books, circulars, outward letters, and so on — together with the dates of these records and the number of items in each series.

Inventories are fuller than series lists. Usually they include an introductory description of a group of records, and indicate the sorts of information to be found in each series. For example, there are published inventories of various collections of papers held by the Alexander Turnbull Library: *Katherine Mansfield: Manuscripts in the Alexander Turnbull Library*, Wellington, 1988; *The Collection of Douglas Lilburn Manuscripts* in the Alexander Turnbull Library, compiled by Jill Palmer, Wellington, 1990; and Cathy Marr's *A Guide to the Archives of the New Zealand Federation of Labour, 1937-88*, Palmerston North, 1988.

Calendars are the most detailed of all. They give an abstract or epitome of each item in a series. Attractive examples of calendars are those for *The Fowlds Papers* in the Auckland University Library, compiled by Frank Rogers, Auckland, 1980.

For most groups and collections, series lists will be available, for a few there will be inventories, but practically none have calendars. For an indication of how libraries arrange these aids, reference can be made to the several publications of the National Archives. The most important guide to a collection, however, is the librarian or archivist who, if experienced, will be able to describe and find relevant material in many likely and unlikely places.

9.2 Published collections of selected documents

Sometimes it is not necessary, at least in the first instance, to delve into unpublished records. Significant collections of documents have been published. For example, a useful general collection of published documents is *Speeches and Documents in New Zealand History*, edited by two historians W. D. McIntyre and W. J. Gardner, Wellington, 1971. Political scientists have produced *New Zealand Politics Source Book*, Palmerston North, 2nd ed. 1994, a volume packed with a variety of legal, political and constitutional information. In photocopied (or, formerly, cyclostyled) form teaching departments at universities have compiled various collections.

'International relations' figures large in the *Politics Source Book* and it is notably in this field, of external relations, that some of the most comprehensive editions of published documents are available. Along with its commissioned volumes covering New Zealand at war, for example, the War History Branch of the Department of Internal Affairs published three volumes of *Documents Relating to New Zealand's Participation in the Second World War 1939-45*, and subsequently the re-named Historical Publications Branch published three volumes in a series of *Documents on New Zealand's External Relations*:

> Vol. 1: *The Australian-New Zealand Agreement 1944*, Wellington, 1972
> Vol. 2: *The Surrender and Occupation of Japan*, Wellington, 1982
> Vol. 3: *The Anzus Pact and the Treaty of Peace with Japan*, Wellington, 1985

These were all edited by Robin Kay. The primary purpose of the series — it was stated — was to make available to scholars at the earliest possible stage documents on the development of New Zealand's foreign policy. There is also the substantial *New Zealand Foreign Policy: Statements and Documents 1943-1957*, Wellington, 1972, produced by the Ministry of Foreign Affairs, and in the post-war years, published documents on the foreign policy of the United States contain New Zealand material. No. 28 in the Canberra Studies in World Affairs, *The Anzus Documents*, ed. Alan Burnett with Thomas-Durell Young and Christine Wilson, Canberra, 1991, is a collection of, or provides references to, defence and security treaties, memoranda and arrangements negotiated by Australia, New Zealand and the United States since 1952.

Various older published collections, although sometimes more detailed, are now used comparatively little, since they follow the traditional orientation of a past generation towards constitutional studies based on official documents:

> R. McNab, ed., *Historical Records of New Zealand*, 2 vols, Wellington, 1908-14
> J. Rutherford et al., compilers, *Select Documents Relative to the Development of Responsible Government in New Zealand ...*, Auckland, 1949 and 1955 (mimeographed)
> D. K. Fieldhouse, ed., *British Colonial Policy in Relation to New Zealand 1871-1902: Documents from the Colonial Office Papers in the Public Record Office*, Christchurch, 1956 (mimeographed)

There is a New Zealand section as well as comparative material in *Select Documents on British Colonial Policy 1830-1860*, ed. K. N. Bell and W. P. Morrell, Oxford, 1928, and similarly useful are:

> A. B. Keith, ed., *Selected Speeches and Documents on British Colonial Policy 1763-1917*, London, 1918
> A. B. Keith, ed., *Speeches and Documents on the British Dominions 1918-1931*, London, 1932
> N. Mansergh, ed., *Documents and Speeches on British Commonwealth Affairs, 1931-1952*, London, 1953

Much early Australian material, some of direct significance to New Zealand history, is published in the voluminous, although never completed, *Historical Records of Australia*, ed. J. F. Watson, 33 vols, Sydney, 1914-22, and the earlier series which it superseded, *Historical Records of New South Wales*, ed. F. M. Bladen, Sydney, 1889-1901.

9.3 Official archives and records: central and local government

The National Archives, a division of the Department of Internal Affairs, is the main repository for government records. To it, sooner or later, government departments pass on their non-current records for storage — or destruction. Note, however, that since politicians and civil servants do not always draw a very precise distinction between personal and official papers, some official records are found in private collections.

Current records, of course, are held by the government departments and state agencies themselves, and for guidance as to what they hold there is the *Directory of Official Information* [above, **7.1.1**]. Although the Official Information Act 1983 gives an inquirer some rights of access, there may well be a fee payable, and sensitive, private, commercial or cabinet-level material may be withheld. An inquirer who appeals to the Ombudsman to recommend release of material cannot be assured of success and may face very considerable delay. For anyone wanting to complete a research study in a limited time, it is better to turn to another topic if material is not readily forthcoming. One of the researcher's friends in the system, it should be remembered, is his or her local M.P.

Post-war development of the **National Archives** under a small and enthusiastic team was described by Pamela S. Cocks in the *Journal of the Society of Archivists* 3 (1966): 121-6. Their work generated a series of *Preliminary Inventories*, 1953-61, which still have value as detailed descriptions of some major categories of papers. Later, for a decade, from 1966, an annual *Summary of Work* was published, culminating in a booklet: *A Cumulative List of Holdings*, 1976. One further *Summary* was published, for 1976/1977. Since then there has been a brief reference to the Archives in the annual report of the Internal Affairs Department in the *Appendices to the Journals of the House of Representatives*, shoulder number G. 7. There are, incidentally, no formalised rules regarding access to official documents deposited in the Archives, such as the British thirty-year rule. [See too **Finding Maori Information: 10.2.1.**]

In pursuit of particular material, however, the researcher may well have to turn to the many institutions outside Wellington. Some produce their own reports, records, bulletins, and so on. Under the Archives Act, 1957, archives which are considered to be unsuitable for the National Archives may be deposited either in the Turnbull Library or in any other library or museum approved by the Minister of Internal Affairs. Provincial libraries and institutions, therefore, may receive and hold not only records generated by local authorities but also records from district offices of the central government — such as land records or magistrates' courts records. However, in recent years as noted above, [**3.1**] National Archives has had offices in Auckland, Christchurch and Dunedin. [On Maori records see too below, **Finding Maori Information: 10**. Note, too, on maps **above 4.5.**]

The bulk of the archives of the provinces which were abolished in 1876 are held in the National Archives, but archives and records of local authorities abolished in more recent years — notably with the local government restructuring of 1989 — have tended to end up in local or regional repositories. A beneficial effect of that restructuring incidentally has been that with the larger and stronger, and better funded, local units of government now in existence, local authorities nowadays increasingly are employing professional archivists to organise their records. But the larger cities, at any rate, will have impressively maintained records dating back to their earliest days.

9.4 Non-government archives: organisations and groups

Note on pictorial and sound and visual recorded material 'Directories and library holdings': 3.2

The writing of centennial and sesquicentennial histories and chronicles has been, and doubtless will continue to be, an incentive to those concerned to make their records available to historians. Archives of business firms and other institutions and societies — labour, religious, musical, political, for example — are frequently not listed or catalogued. The material must be dug out, and access and use are by the grace and favour of the holder. As a result, tactless approaches by an inquirer, or unauthorised publication of material, may cause an institution to close its files to all researchers.

A few business houses have deposited their records in libraries, but in many cases business archives in New Zealand have been woefully deficient (— see J. A. Ellis's *Business Archives in New Zealand*, Wellington, 1975). By scanning through the various Company Acts, it is possible to see what records registered companies were required to keep at different times. Most business houses will keep records of accounts, and larger firms at least are likely to preserve minutes of directors' meetings. Law firms always tend to keep their old records.

The profession of archivist has made great strides in the past twenty to thirty years; although relatively few in number — there were 81 people listed in the *Directory of Archivists in New Zealand 1990-91*, compiled by Mark H. S. Stevens, Wellington, 1990 — archivists have nonetheless managed to exercise some pressure, and influence, in the right places. Companies and organisations have been persuaded to donate their records to local or national repositories; some major businesses have appointed their own archivists, as also have other corporate bodies, like the Society of Mary. Several major churches have established formal national archival repositories, as well as the repositories at diocesan level of episcopal churches.

The Turnbull Library is developing a co-ordinated policy of collecting religious archives in conjunction with the appropriate denominations, church bodies and other repositories. An inventory for its manuscript papers is available. Some of the unpublished records of churches which sent missions to the Maori in the first decades of European contact are available in New Zealand. A microfilm of the Church Missionary Society's archives relating to the Australian and the New Zealand missions is held in the Turnbull and Hocken Libraries (see the Church Missionary Society's *Guide to the Microfilmed Archives relating to the Australian and New Zealand Missions, 1808-1884* [1959], typescript). The Methodist Missionary Society archives are held in microfilm by the Hocken and Turnbull Libraries, and the Turnbull Library also has a microfilm of New Zealand material from the Marist Archives in Rome (see the description of the Archives by Hugh Laracy in the *Journal of Pacific History* 3 (1968): 165-71, 5 (1970): 158-9).

In honour of International Women's Year (1975), the Alexander Turnbull Library established the New Zealand Women's History Research Collection, which has built on the library's existing manuscript holdings with material from individual women and from women's organisations (for example, records of the National Council of Women and of the Women's Christian Temperance Union). Another example of burgeoning interest in developing resource centres — and the implicit political significance of such centres — is the Lesbian and Gay Rights Resource Centre, established in Wellington in 1977 and now in the Alexander Turnbull Library. Not surprisingly, considering that homosexuality between males was not decriminalised until the late 1980s, the centre has little material which precedes the 1960s.

As previously noted [3.2], the Peace Movement Aotearoa has published a *Bibliography of Peace Archives*, Wellington, 1991.

In addition to unpublished archives, there is a wealth of material in the published records of companies, political parties, trade unions, churches, and other organisations and interest groups, in their newspapers and journals, annual reports, and proceedings of regional and national conferences and assemblies. Two outstanding examples from New Zealand colonial history are the *Reports* (London, 1840-58) of the London-based New Zealand Company (the archives of which are in the National Archives), and publications of missionary societies, particularly the *Church Missionary Record*, London, 1830-90. There is a guide to *Collections of Religion and Theology in Australia and New Zealand*, compiled by Coralie Jenkin, Adelaide, 1994. [Mentioned above **9.1** is *Guide to the Archives of the New Zealand Federation of Labour*. An inventory is available for the archives in Wellington of the major state sector union, the Public Service Association.]

9.5 Broadcasting and film

Official newsreels on New Zealand have been produced since 1907. New Zealand and overseas films dating back to 1897 are held by the New Zealand Film Archive, established in Wellington in 1981, whose film searches through the country since 1992 have discovered hundreds of old New Zealand films now deposited in the Archive. Regrettably, no catalogues have been compiled, although the Archive has published a newsletter (1981-96), and a brief report (1998). Its admission in 1985 as full member of the Fédération Internationale des Archives du Film (founded 1938) indicates the high standards achieved by the Archive. Viewing and research fees are charged, and researchers are advised to make prior appointment (contact: The Director, The New Zealand Film Archive, P. O. Box 9544, Wellington).

National Archives is the official repository for film produced by government agencies, most notably the National Film Unit. The National Archives also holds government files relating to theatre licensing and censorship. The National Film Unit had a card file of its productions, including its weekly newsreels which it produced for many years from 1941. For films held for use in schools by the National Film Library (now part of the National Library), see the National Film Library *Film & Video Catalogue*, Wellington, 1989 and its *Supplement*, 1991. [See too **Finding Maori Information: 10.4.1.**]

At Foxton, in the old Foxton theatre, is the Audio Visual Arts and Science Museum which, by the mid 1990s, as well as old cinema projectors and ancient gramophones, had built up a collection of 15 million feet of film and about 200,000 records, disks and cylinders.

Broadcasting in New Zealand dates from the 1920s: see Patrick Day's *The Radio Years: a history of broadcasting in New Zealand*, Auckland, 1994. A fully-fledged radio news service dates from 1962, coinciding with broadcasting passing from a government department to a corporation: a move associated with the introduction of television to the four main centres in the years 1960-62. There are more than 50,000 acetate discs, tapes, and commercial recordings in the Radio New Zealand Sound Archives in Christchurch (formerly in Timaru), established in 1956. Original recordings date from the 1930s and, with transcriptions from old recordings, the period covered stretches back to reminiscences of the early years of European settlement. See the two large volumes of *Sounds Historical: A Catalogue of the Sound History Recordings in the Sound Archives of Radio New Zealand, Timaru,* Timaru, 1982. The Archives also has published *A Catalogue of Recordings made by the New Zealand Mobile Broadcasting Unit in the Pacific theatre of war during World War Two, April 1943 to August 1944*, and a similar *Catalogue* for North Africa and Europe, both compiled by Norman C. Batty, Christchurch, 1996. Paper archives of past national radio are held in the National Archives.

Radio New Zealand's Replay Radio also retails cassettes drawing upon its archives, such as 'Great Moments in New Zealand History', or 'Good Morning Everybody', the latter containing sample programmes of Aunt Daisy. A book, *Snapshots of the Century: Spectrum covers 100 years of New Zealand History*, edited by Alwyn Owen, 1998, is a selection from some one thousand documentaries broadcast since 1972. [See too above **3.2**: Oral records.]

The New Zealand Television Archive was set up as an independent commercial archive to preserve film from all New Zealand television companies. The Archive has a computer database of news items and also indexes other New Zealand television programmes.

9.6 Personal papers

The main repositories of personal papers are the Turnbull and Hocken Libraries. But to tap the wealth of collections of private papers the researcher will need to travel around New Zealand, or beyond, using guides and catalogues such as the *National Register of Archives and Manuscripts*, the *Union Catalogue of Manuscripts* and catalogues of individual libraries, to track down relevant material in library collections. In some cases, too, one will need to approach private individuals in a quest for unlisted family papers. It is through such initiative that some major privately-held collections have come into library hands.

Ideally, unpublished material should be studied in the original; copies are always subject to errors and omissions — a human weakness which constantly bedevils a scholar's own notes, and which scholars forget at their peril. In the case of massive collections of printed official documents, of course, it is neither feasible nor necessary to turn to the original manuscript copies — even if they are available. With collections of private papers, also, much time can be wasted if transcripts and published versions are ignored. For example, much of the Turnbull Library's collection of papers of Edward William Stafford, the early New Zealand politician, has been typed, incorrectly in many details but at least legibly. Time is gained if typescript and original letters are used in conjunction. G. H. Scholefield edited a selection of the massive collection of the nineteenth-century *Richmond-Atkinson Papers*, the bulk of which was then held in the General Assembly (Parliamentary) Library. In Scholefield's two-volume edition (Wellington, 1960), the material is sorted out and indexed — but it is also very incomplete. Such publications, of which this is the largest and most important, are therefore of use primarily for quick reference, and as a guide to the contents of a collection.

Various other collections of early letters have also been published — not necessarily in so massive a form — for example, *Letters of Thomas Arnold the Younger ...*, ed. James Bertram, Auckland, 1966. A later example is *Na to Hoa Aroha/From your Dear Friend: The Correspondence between Sir Apirana Ngata and Sir Peter Buck, 1925-50*, ed. M. P. K. Sorrenson, 3 vols, Auckland, 1986-88. Ian McGibbon has edited *Undiplomatic Dialogue Letters between Carl Berendsen and Alister McIntosh 1943-1952*, Auckland, 1993. The most comprehensive edition of the letters of Katherine Mansfield is

Katherine Mansfield, Selected Letters, edited by Vincent O'Sullivan, Oxford, 1989. In addition, several journals have been published: there is a two-volume edition of *The Katherine Mansfield Notebooks*, edited by Margaret Scott, Wellington, 1997. An outstanding example is *The Journals of Captain James Cook on his Voyages of Discovery*, ed. J. C. Beaglehole, 4 vols in 5, Cambridge, 1955-1974, in which a great wealth of material on New Zealand may be found. Covering only a short span of New Zealand history, but a good example of the work of the diarist, is *The Journal of Henry Sewell 1853-7*, ed. W. D. McIntyre, 2 vols, Christchurch, 1980. J. R. Elder edited *The Letters and Journals of Samuel Marsden, 1765-1838*, Dunedin, 1932 (as well as *Marsden's Lieutenants*, Dunedin, 1934).

These are the works of professional academics, and include examples of the highest standards of modern and meticulous scholarship, such as most editors cannot match. Nevertheless, used with discretion, the continuing stream of edited letters, journals, diaries, and memoirs in print can provide the researcher with valuable material, readily accessible.

9.7 Archives and manuscripts held overseas

For years the *Calendar* of a New Zealand university, or university college,[1] listed prescribed texts for the various courses. Later course lists may be available in cyclostyled or photocopied form. Those old course descriptions and their prescribed texts are a valuable source for finding the world, a heavily eurocentric world, that New Zealanders used to know and study. As New Zealanders grappled with problems of national identity, long since rejecting an identity as an off-shoot of Britain, and on the periphery of British culture, by the last years of the twentieth century they had turned again to European roots as well as to Polynesian. For example the journal *Antipodes*, 1995–, is devoted to study of contacts between New Zealand and the French-speaking world. Increasingly, too, New Zealanders recognised also the other components of New Zealand development, such as the Chinese contribution, especially in gold-rush areas. There are significant remnants of the past held in New Zealand institutions — in art, artefacts, and manuscript. As well as published documents, some unpublished British and Australian sources are available in New Zealand — or at least, in the case of Australia, within reasonably easy access to the New Zealand researcher. For example, there is a bibliography of *Medieval and Renaissance Manuscripts in New Zealand Collections*, by Margaret M. Manion, Vera Frances Vines, and Christopher Francis Rivers De Hamel, Melbourne, 1989.

---

1 See note #1, **8.l.**

Before the formal assumption of British sovereignty over New Zealand in 1840, there were decades when the islands were within the British sphere of influence, or likely to become so; from the foundation of Sydney in the late eighteenth century, Governors in New South Wales had a vague responsibility for this area of the Pacific. Australian records are indispensable for study of this facet of New Zealand history. The massive published series, the *Historical Records of Australia*, has been mentioned above [**9.2**]. There are also available in New Zealand, in the National Archives, microfilms of New Zealand interest from the Archives Office of New South Wales and from the research collections in the State Library of New South Wales. For particular areas of research a New Zealander may find of value material in the archives of other Australian states. The Public Record Office of Victoria, for example, has details of gold-rush emigration to Otago.

There are guides to unpublished Australian material, of which the most useful is probably the well-indexed guide to the holdings of the Mitchell Library, *Catalogue of Manuscripts of Australasia and the Pacific in the Mitchell Library, Sydney*, Sydney, 1967–. So far, parts A and B have been published, listing manuscripts, including New Zealand material, accessioned in the years 1945 to 1967. A microfilm copy of the catalogue of pre-1945 accessions is held in libraries.

The National Library of Australia, *Guide to Collections of Manuscripts Relating to Australia*, Canberra, 1965–, is a loose-leaf production, with indexes to all personal and corporate names. Since 1985 it has been superseded by a similarly-titled selective union list, on microfiche. Olga White, Anne Marie Schwirtlich, and Jennifer Nash have produced *Our Heritage: A Directory to Archives and Manuscript Repositories in Australia*, Canberra, 1983. *Australian Historical Studies* provides useful occasional notifications of library accessions of manuscripts, and the *Journal of Pacific History* has valuable reports on manuscript holdings.

Specifically on British manuscripts, the two most important guides are:

- Phyllis Mander-Jones, *Manuscripts in the British Isles Relating to Australia, New Zealand, and the Pacific,* Canberra, 1972

- *Guide to the Contents of the Public Record Office*, 3 vols, London, 1963-68, and subsequently on microfiche

A useful little book on British documents and repositories is *Record Repositories in Great Britain*, 10th ed., London, 1998. The British Library is producing an *Index of Manuscripts in the British Library,* Cambridge, 1984–. As with all major libraries, information about the British Library is on the Internet. http://minos.bl.uk/index.htm — and from its site there are links to other libraries, such as the Library of Congress in the United States.

There are chapters on Australian and New Zealand material in the United Kingdom in *Australian and New Zealand Studies: Papers Presented at a Colloquium at the British Library 7-9 February 1984,* ed. Patricia McLaren-Turner, London, 1985. Also helpful are such specialised guides as:

Rosemary Keen, *A Survey of the Archives of Selected Missionary Societies,* 5th ed., London, 1973

Charles A. Jones, *Britain and the Dominions: A Guide to Business and Related Records in the United Kingdom concerning Australia, Canada, New Zealand and South Africa,* Boston, 1978

Margaret Barrow, *Women, 1870-1928: A Select Guide to Printed and Archival Sources in the United Kingdom,* London, 1981

A major source of early New Zealand political and constitutional history is the series of dispatches exchanged between New Zealand Governors and the British authorities, normally the Colonial Office, spiced with marginal notes and minutes added by officials at each end. Indeed, on these sources has been built the whole structure of British colonial and commonwealth history until recent years. R. B. Pugh's *The Records of the Colonial and Dominion Office* (Public Record Office Handbook No. 3), London, 1964, is a first-class work with an invaluable introductory section on the administrative processes that created the records of this office.

The National Archives holds both the Governors' copies of dispatches and, for the nineteenth century, microfilm of the copies in the Public Record Office in London: a useful complement to the New Zealand holdings, since they contain the office notes on which replies were based. Indeed, under a Joint Copying Project initiated by two Australian libraries after the war, all Public Record Office material relevant to the history of Australia, New Zealand and the Pacific is being microfilmed and made available for purchase by New Zealand libraries, led by the National Archives. The *Australian Joint Copying Project Handbook,* Canberra, 1972– (2nd ed., 1984–), provides a description of all the microfilming done to date, as well as listing some of the holdings of different libraries. If Colonial Office records have been used in particular by political and constitutional historians, the *Handbook* of the Joint Copying Project, and the associated Mander-Jones *Manuscripts in the British Isles* (cited above), show just how wide is the range of material available in Britain for pursuing New Zealand studies.

There is also significant material of relevance to New Zealand study in other government archives. Inter-governmental exchanges are an obvious example: scholars' ability to view overseas government material sometimes has enabled them to circumvent restrictions on access imposed at home by their own governments. Of different character are comments and reports: for example, reports on early New Zealand were sent to their home governments by naval officers and others (see Leslie R. Marchant, 'The French Discovery and Settlement of New Zealand, 1769-1846: A Bibliographical Essay on Naval Records in Paris,' *Historical Studies*, 10 (1963): 511-18). In addition, there are consular and diplomatic reports on New Zealand, happily not all of the 'staggering ineptitude' of some American consulate reports during the second world war.[1] Microfilm copies of reports of the United States consul for the first fifty years of British settlement in New Zealand are held in the National Archives. For the United States, there are

> *Directory of Archives and Manuscript Repositories in the United States*, Washington, 1978

> *National Union Catalog of Manuscript Collections*, 1962–.

The Canadians have a

> *Directory of Canadian Archives*, ed. Marcel Caya and others, Ottawa, 1986

> *Union List of Manuscripts in Canadian Repositories*, Ottawa, 1975, with several *Supplements,* 1976–

Since 1972 the International Council on Archives has published several volumes in *Guides to the Sources for the History of the Nations: 3rd Series, North Africa, Asia and Oceania*, including:

> vol. 1: *Guide des Sources de l'Histoire d'Afrique du Nord, d'Asie et d'Océanie Conservées en Belgique*, ed. Emile Vandewoude and André Vanrie. 1972.

> vol. 2: *Sources de l'Histoire de l'Asie et de l'Océanie dans les Archives et Bibliothèques Françaises*, ed. Commission Française du Guide des

---

1 F. L. W. Wood, reviewing *New Zealand Becomes a Pacific Power* by B. K. Gordon, Chicago, 1960, in *Political Science*, 13 (1961): 94: 'Gordon quotes ... two extracts from American consulate reports ... of such staggering ineptitude as to raise irreverent speculation as to what American consuls write home when stationed in non-English speaking countries.'

Sources de l'Histoire des Nations. Part I: *Archives*. 1981. Part 2: *Bibliothèque Nationale*. 1981.

vol. 3: *Sources of the History of North Africa, Asia and Oceania in Scandinavia*. Part 1: *Sources ... in Denmark*, ed. C. Rise Hansen. 1980. Part 2: *Sources ... in Finland, Norway and Sweden*, ed. B. Federley et al. 1981.

vol. 4: *Sources of the History of Asia and Oceania in the Netherlands*. Part I: *Sources up to 1796*, ed. Marius P. H. Roessingh. 1982. Part II: *Sources 1796-1949*, ed. Fritz G. Jaquet. 1983.

vol. 6: *Quellen zur Geschichte Nordafrikas, Asiens und Ozeaniens in der Bundesrepublik Deutschland bis 1945*, ed. Ernst Ritter. 1984.

vol. 8: *Quellen zur Geschichte Afrikas, Asiens und Ozeaniens im Österreichischen Staatsarchiv bis 1918*. 1986.

vol. 9: *Sources of the History of Africa, Asia, Australia and Oceania in Hungary: with a supplement: Latin America*. 1991.

Vol. 10: *Sources of the History of Africa, Asia and Oceania in Yugoslavia*, ed. Vereinigung der Gesellschaften der Archivare in Jugoslawien. 1990.

These volumes are inventories of the contents of national and other archives in the countries concerned. The first (Belgian) volume is published by the Archives Générales du Royaume, the remainder by the firm of K. G. Saur (Munich, London, New York, Paris).

The International Council on Archives also publishes from time to time an *International Directory of Archives/Annuaire International des Archives*, as a volume of *Archivum*, such as volume 38, 1992.

10. Finding Maori Information

by Kirsten Stewart[1]

Note also references to 'Maori' information in the Index. 'Te' and 'Nga' = 'The', 'He' = 'A' or 'An', and may not be used in title indexes or catalogues.

This is not intended as a comprehensive guide to all the bibliographies on Maori resources which have been compiled, but rather, as a selective summary of the more comprehensive, important or less obvious bibliographies which are useful as a starting point for the researcher. As with the rest of this book, rather than listing direct information sources the intention has been to guide users towards the tools or bibliographies which will then lead them to the sources. Therefore researchers' attention is drawn to those categories not included. Notable sources are: monographs with extensive bibliographies such as Claudia Orange's *The Treaty of Waitangi*, Wellington, 1992, and the various tribal histories; government reports on Maori such as sections of *The April Report: Report of the Royal Commission on Social Policy*, Wellington, 1988 [cf above **2.2**]; the *Hunn Report* [*Report on the Department of Maori Affairs ... 24 August 1960*, by J. K. Hunn, Wellington, 1961, also published in the *Appendices to the Journals of the House of Representatives*]; *Ka Awatea*; *a Report of the Ministerial Planning Group*, Wellington, 1991; and the Raupatu [land confiscations] document bank — for example *Te Raupatu o Tauranga Moana. Vol. 2, Documents relating to tribal history, confiscation and reallocation of Tauranga lands*,

---

1   This essay by Kirsten Stewart has been slightly re-arranged and edited.

compiled and edited by Evelyn Stokes, Hamilton, 1993 — and *Reports* of the Waitangi Tribunal [cf above **2.1**].

10.1 Research collections

Some Maori manuscripts and resources are held in private hands and are not publicly available. To locate Maori primary material which is publicly available in New Zealand collections a good starting point is

> • Chris Szekely, *Te Hikoi Marama: A Directory of Maori Information Resources*, Wellington, updated edition 1993.

Arranged geographically, from North to South, the directory lists not only libraries but museums, publishing groups, resource centres, research teams, and a variety of other organisations, giving details of the nature of their collections or services, including hours open and contact persons. There is a brief description of collections and the type of access available. Excellent additional access is provided through the indexes: a general index, a subject index and an index to organisations.

For more detail than available in *Te Hikoi Marama*, there is the *National Register of Archives and Manuscripts in New Zealand* [**9.1**]. Other general guides worth checking include: *Archives New Zealand 3* and *4*, compiled and edited by Frank Rogers, Plimmerton, 1990 and 1992 [**10.1**], and, for items held outside New Zealand, Phyllis Mander-Jones, ed. *Manuscripts in the British Isles relating to Australia, New Zealand and the Pacific*, Canberra, 1972 [**9.7**]. For oral history collections check the National Oral History Association of New Zealand's *Oral History in New Zealand: a directory of collections 1992*, Wellington, 1992 [**3.2**].

10.2 Guides to specific collections

10.2.1 National Archives

As the main repository for government records, the National Archives is the repository for letters written by Maori to Governors, surveyors and government departments, and for the records of the Native, later Maori, Land Courts which include the minute books and the accompanying documents from the land court offices. Other record series are also of interest for Maori research — for example records of the Department of Internal Affairs and Maori Affairs Department (for decades Native Affairs Department) and its successors: Ministry of Maori Affairs, Iwi Transition Agency and Te Puni Kokiri. Note, however, that from 1989 there has been 'mainstreaming' of Maori affairs, with the replacement of the Maori Affairs Department/Ministry;

the Ministry of Maori Development, Te Puni Kokiri, is a slimmed-down solely policy unit.

National Archives has published a good general guide: *A Guide to Maori Sources at National Archives = He Pukaki Maori:Te Whare Tohu Tuhituhinga o Aotearoa*, Wellington, 1995. *He Pukaki Maori* includes a brief guide to research prior to the material being transferred to the National Archives, and lists relevant published sources of information. Then it is divided into research topics for information held at National Archives: genealogy, land and war. It also includes a list of 'Other research topics': health, culture, politics, women, etc. For each topic the type of information which is likely to be of value is detailed along with series codes. There is no additional indexing. The guide is not as detailed as other more specific inventories and leaflets which are available on request from National Archives such as *Some strategies for searching Maori names and land blocks: some suggestions for searching Maori names and land blocks at National Archives*, National Archives Reference Guide No. 16, which outlines what to do if you know the Maori name or the name of the block and details the file codes in use at Archives.

As research into land claims and interest in Maori topics has increased, other organisations have also tried to improve access to Maori information. An important source created to enhance access to the Land Court Minute Books is John Laurie, 'Index to Minute Books of the Maori Land Court 1865-1910' in which 'hearings are indexed by block name, witnesses names, type of case, length of case, place of sitting, whakapapa and hapu'. It is held as a computer file accessible at the University of Auckland library. The index is in progress.

Another index to the court minute books is the Department of Maori Affairs, *Maori Land Court Minute Books Microfilmed: A record and index of minute books 1865 to 1900*, Wellington, 1961[?], a printed inventory consisting of a numerical list of the reels and their contents. It also includes an index to the Maori Land Court Minute books. Organised by land court district, each entry details the place of sitting, microfilm reference number, the place and dates of sittings and the judge. The Turnbull Library copy includes a pencil note that National Archives have more recent indexes from 1900.

The microfilms for the Maori Land Court Minute Books: New Zealand 1865-1906, and Tai Tokerau 1900-1962 are available. The Alexander Turnbull Library also holds the index, in a folder, to Tai Tokerau and the indexes to the following microfilms held by National Archives. All the indexes are arranged in the same way as noted above. National Archives has copies on microfilm of Vol. 3 Waikato-Maniapoto, Vol. 4 Waiariki, Vol. 5 Tairawhiti, Vol. 6 Aotea, Vol. 7 Ikaroa, Vol. 8 South Island. Indexes to these are available at the Alexander Turnbull Library manuscripts room.

10.2.2 Alexander Turnbull Library

Among the resources of the Alexander Turnbull Library may be noted its holdings of nineteenth-century newspapers, the papers of the Polynesian Society, and the papers of Pakeha involved with, or interested in Maori, such as William Colenso, Sir Donald McLean, W. B. D. Mantell, John White, Elsdon Best, and John Houston. The Turnbull Library also has a copy of all the manuscripts in the Sir George Grey collection in the Auckland Public Library (other copies are at the Auckland University and Canterbury University libraries).

The main access tools at the Turnbull Library are the [above **3.2**] computer file Tapuhi, and the card catalogues. Both are currently available in the manuscripts room of the Library. Tapuhi contains information about the collections of unpublished material held in the Turnbull Library. Tapuhi is not comprehensive and it is still necessary to use the card catalogue, although new items are all entered on the database and older items are being entered retrospectively. The Turnbull Library is also preparing an index to Maori newspapers.

A useful outline of the type of information relevant to Maori studies held at the Alexander Turnbull Library and an excellent starting point for researching Maori information at the Library is *Etahi o nga taonga Maori,Turnbull Library Record* 23(1) 1990. This whole issue of the *Record* is devoted to a 'series of articles written by staff members and users of the collections describing the major resources for Maori studies in the Turnbull with particular emphasis on the Maori language materials'. It includes articles on Maori language printed collections, niupepa, maps, and using the Turnbull Library to research Maori women.

10.2.3 National Library of New Zealand

Access to resources of the National Library is through the online catalogue. The Library's Maori resources have been collected together into a reference area in the reading room, and another important access tool is *Rauemi Tuhi: Maori Resource Guide*, 3rd ed. Wellington, 1994, an unpublished typescript held on the display shelves. References made are to published information only — the guide excludes material held in the collection of the Alexander Turnbull Library. It is arranged in five sections: Maori Tribal History, Maori Culture and Traditions, Maori Serials, Maori Audio-Visual Material, Maori Biographical Sources. The serials and audio-visual material bibliographies have brief annotations. The others consist of bibliographical details only.

10.2.4 Auckland City Libraries

Auckland Public Library holds the Sir George Grey collection, including letters, waiata, korero and whakapapa. It also holds the Te

Rangikaheke manuscripts, as well as the papers of Shortland, Taylor and Colenso.

Access is provided through a computer file called Iwidex, the database for the Library's New Zealand and Pacific sources and held in its New Zealand and Pacific Department. It is an index to information on iwi appearing in manuscripts (for example the Grey Maori manuscripts), books, periodicals and newspapers articles. It is still being updated and the main emphasis is on historical information. It is intended to publish in print in sections. Volume 1, the first of these, is *Ngapuhi*, the work of Patricia French, Robin Hakopa, and others, Auckland, 1993.

10.2.5 Hocken Library

Relatively small but significant manuscript collections with a particular emphasis on the Kai Tahu are held by the Hocken Library among the papers of F. R. Chapman, J. F. H. Wohlers and Herries Beattie, with wider geographic coverage among Edward Shortland's notebooks. The journals of the early Church Missionary Society missionaries provide insight into early Maori-Pakeha relations in the Bay of Islands and the Far North. Access to the manuscript collection is available through Hakena, the Library's database. Much material, such as Maori Land Court minute books and missionary society archives, is held on microfilm. Published collections are comprehensive.

10.3 Guides to doing Maori research

The following books have been published as introductory guides to doing research on Maori topics. Although they are specific to tribal history and land claims, they are valuable for anyone doing research in the area as they outline resources available, techniques and problems.

• Charles Royal, *Te Haurapa: an introduction to researching tribal histories and traditions*, Wellington, 1992

outlines problems and issues to be aware of when doing tribal research, and also discusses the types of material which are available: manuscripts and books, paintings, maps, photos, films, videos and sound tapes. For recorded information the holding institutions are listed along with a list of some specific sources useful for research on Maori topics.

• Jane Tucker, *Maori Claims: how to research and write a report*, Waitangi Tribunal occasional publication 1/1994. Wellington, 1994 is divided into six sections with a short bibliography relating to research guides and research directories at the end. Tucker broadly outlines the types of sources holding information pertinent to land claims. Specific institutions such as National Archives are detailed — this includes how to access the information, costs and locations. It is a very useful basic guide for the novice researcher.

• *Te Ara Tirohanga: a guide for researchers into Maori claims*, Waitangi Tribunal occasional publication No. 3, rev. ed., Wellington, 1993.

Divided into five main sections this guide describes the groups involved in the claim process. Sections four and five list sources of information. These include government departments as well as libraries and archives. Addresses, access and collection details are noted: publicity-leaflet type style. The guide pulls together the institutions holding information required for land claims and also details locations. Less a guide to carrying out the actual research than a list of relevant places to go.

10.3.1 Electronic access to Maori information

Electronic sources fall into two main access categories. Those locally held, to access which it is necessary to visit the holding, usually the creating, institution, and those available through the Internet which can be searched from other locations: many library catalogues now are available. The most useful, up-to-date summary of Maori electronic sources available is an article written by Alastair G. Smith and Robert Sullivan, 'Maori electronic information: issues and resources', *New Zealand Libraries*, 48(6) June 1996. This details the issues surrounding electronic access and also the resources available. An updated version is available on the Internet:

• 'Fishing with New Nets: Maori Internet Information Resources and Implications of the Internet for Indigenous Peoples', www.isoc.org/inet97/proceedings/E1/E1_1.HTM.

10.4 Bibliographies

10.4.1 New Zealand bibliographies: general

Note 'New Zealand bibliographies': 5.1.1

For publications up to 1960, the major bibliographical guide for New Zealand works is, of course, A. G. Bagnall, *New Zealand National Bibliography to the year 1960* [5.1.1]. The chronological and separate author/subject/title indexes can be used for locating monographs on Maori topics. For specific subject search for items published after

1889 and up to 1960 it is necessary to check the subject index included in Volume 5. For items published after 1960 check the *New Zealand National Bibliography* on paper and then on microfiche, and the New Zealand Bibliographic Network or Te Puna [2.2].

T. M. Hocken's *A Bibliography of the Literature relating to New Zealand* [5.1.1] remains of value to the researcher despite being superseded for Maori language items by H. W. Williams' *Bibliography of Printed Maori to 1900* [below 10.4.3] and for English language monographs by Bagnall's *New Zealand National Bibliography*. The detailed subject index to Hocken's *Bibliography* refers to many items written about the Maori dating from the 1830s, and is particularly useful for the ephemeral items included. A. H. Johnstone, *Supplement to Hocken's Bibliography of New Zealand literature*, Wellington, 1927, also lists Maori topics in the subject index.

An important source to check for Maori bibliographical publications, as it includes computer files which are not necessarily published in print format, as well as bibliographies published in journals, is (previously cited, above [5.3]) A. P. U. Millett and F. T. H. Cole, *Bibliographical Work in New Zealand ...: Work in Progress and Work Published*, Hamilton, 1980–. Access to bibliographies on Maori topics from 1986 is through the subject index. (Prior to this there is no subject access; therefore it is necessary to check all the titles.) Note however that some of the items in this publication are never published, or not necessarily ever published in print.

Derek A. Dow, compiler, *Annotated Bibliography for the History of Health and Medicine in New Zealand* [5.3.1: Health and welfare] is divided into broad subject categories which include Maori **health**. For anyone interested in Maori **religion** and religious movements an important bibliography is Peter J. Lineham and Anthony R. Grigg, *Religious History of New Zealand: a Bibliography* [5.3.1: Religion]. It includes a classified index to Maori religion and missions. A **regional** work providing information about the contents of books which is unavailable elsewhere is *Bibliography of the Waikato Region*, ed. R. C. Hallett and A. P. U. Millett [5.3.1: Regional studies].

10.4.2 New Zealand bibliographies: arts and culture

Eugene C. Burt ed., *Oceanic Art: a Five Year Cumulative Bibliography, mid 1983 through 1988*, Seattle, 1990

brings together all Oceanic art-related items which appeared in the first six volumes of the *Ethnoarts Index*, covering the period from July 1 1983 to December 31 1988. It is divided regionally and has a New Zealand section which lists 131 items. The work includes journal articles, monographs and catalogues, and some items are annotated.

This can be a useful starting point for anyone with an interest in Maori art and artefacts. But note the limited date range.
According to the compilers,

> Louise and F. Allan Hanson, *The Art of Oceania: a Bibliography*, Boston, 1984

'is a bibliography treating the visual arts of Oceania'. It includes monographs, catalogues, theses, dissertations and periodical literature. Except for theses and dissertations, unpublished works are not included, nor are articles in newspapers or, for the most part, museum annual reports. The *Bibliography* is divided by region, with a cross-region section which may contain items of interest on Maori art: New Zealand is included in the Polynesia section. Items are organised alphabetically by author. There are separate personal name, title and subject indexes. In the subject index New Zealand is further divided by the type of art: motifs, baskets, bone, carving, architecture, etc. It seems fairly comprehensive and is an important source for anyone interested in traditional Maori art. It includes items from sources such as *Te Ao Hou, Journal of the Polynesian Society.*

> *Books & Pamphlets relating to Culture and the Arts in New Zealand: A Bibliography Including Works Published to the End of the Year 1977*, compiled by Bernard W. Smyth and Hilary Howorth, Christchurch, 1978

is divided into Culture, Arts, Language and Literature, Communication, Libraries and Archives. The authors note that many items have been excluded from the bibliography as they were considered beyond its scope or because their content was found in another included work. The work does not include periodicals. It contains a significant amount of items with Maori content: the culture, arts, and language and literature categories include sections on Maori music, sculpture, carving, architecture, etc. All items have brief annotations. There is an index of authors/editors and compilers and a subject index with a large number of references under 'Maori'.
The scope of

> Norman Simms, *Writers from the South Pacific: a Bio-bibliographical critical encyclopaedia*, Washington, 1991, *Part II Who's who: supplement.* Working draft 12, February 1993

includes 'more than literary authors in the strict sense of poets, short story writers, novelists, dramatists and essayists. Also looking for script-writers, song-writers, composers of hymns and chants, and others involved in all forms of literary endeavour'. It is organised alphabetically by author; however one can locate Maori authors using this.

> Nicholas J. Goetzfridt, *Indigenous Literature of Oceania: A survey of criticism and interpretation*, Westport, 1995

is divided by region; the bibliography includes a general Oceania section and separate sections on Aotearoa-New Zealand, Pacific Islands, and Australia. The scope is confined to works of poetry, fiction and drama written in English by indigenous peoples of the South Pacific. The main bibliography consists of works of criticism taken from items published in academic and literary journals and books. Divided by geographic region, then by type of work (anthologies, drama, novels, poetry, short fiction). There is an author and title index, a critics index and a subject index. Includes 171 New Zealand items. All items included are annotated. An important source for anyone interested in Maori literature.

In the specialist field of Maori **music**, see

> Mervyn McLean, *An Annotated Bibliography of Oceanic Music and Dance*, 2nd ed., Warren, 1995.

'Entries include references to books, journal articles, reviews, LP recordings, manuscripts on file, theses in commonly read European languages. Mainly excludes dictionaries, song texts in translation, collections of songs with piano accompaniment, publications consisting of words and music of acculturated songs or hymns and newspaper articles'. All entries are arranged alphabetically and chronologically by author, and there is an area index which has a listing under Maori. References to Maori are interspersed amongst the general Oceania references which makes looking them up tedious. However the information is there despite the access difficulties.

Note, too

> *Traditional Songs of the Maori*, by Mervyn E. McLean and Margaret Orbell, rev. ed., Wellington, 1990.

Mervyn McLean has also edited *Catalogue of Radio New Zealand recordings of Maori events, 1938-1950*, Auckland, 1991, for the University of Auckland Archive of Maori and Pacific Music.

10.4.3 Maori bibliographies.

Note 'Newspapers': 6.2

For a comprehensive list of Maori bibliographies (to January 1996) see 'A Bibliography of Guides to Maori Information' by Kirsten Stewart, unpublished research paper, Victoria University of Wellington, 1996, available from the Victoria University Library.

- H. W. Williams, *A Bibliography of Printed Maori to 1900*, and *Supplement*, Wellington, 1924 and 1928; reprinted 1975

is the definitive bibliography of Maori-language publications: 'any work, however small, printed wholly in Maori, or in Maori with a translation, has been admitted; so also any work dealing wholly with the Maori language — as, for example, a dictionary. Excludes works of which only a portion is in Maori'. Entries are based on sighted items and those listed in reliable sources, and are arranged in chronological order, except for series which are kept together for convenience. Undated items have been put in probable chronological place. Each item has brief descriptive notes as well as bibliographical information. There is also a separate index to authors and translators, to printers, to places of origin and to English and Maori titles. The *Supplement* gives items located after publication of the original bibliography in 1924 as well as corrections of errors. The *Supplement* has a separate index and should be used in conjunction with the main index.

A. D. Sommerville, 'A supplement to the Williams bibliography of printed Maori', Wellington, 1947, an unpublished typescript, covers all material printed in Maori from 1900 to 1947, as well as pre-1900 items missed from the Williams' *Bibliography* (although the author did not recheck the *Appendices to the Journals of the House of Representatives* for pre-1900 material). It is arranged in chronological order like Williams, continues the numerical sequence, and is indexed by titles and by author/editor/translator. There are brief descriptive notes for some items.

- C. R. H. Taylor, *A Bibliography of Publications on the New Zealand Maori and Moriori of the Chatham Islands*, Oxford, 1972

is a revised and updated version of the New Zealand and Maori sections of his earlier *A Pacific Bibliography: Printed Matter Relating to the Native Peoples of Polynesia, Melanesia, and Micronesia*, 2nd ed., Oxford, 1965. Divided into broad subject areas, it lists all the books and periodical articles published in these areas. It includes a detailed author/subject index. Taylor notes that the listing is not a definitive record as it does not include ephemeral items. Nevertheless, despite its age and this exclusion Taylor's *Bibliography* remains the most comprehensive available. Note that many of the bibliographies listed in it have been superseded since publication in 1972.

- University of Waikato Library, New Zealand Collection Librarians, *Maori Bibliography* — telnet to: library.waikato.ac.nz (username: OPAC)

is particularly strong on Maori history and culture. Publication is not intended but it is maintained as an updated computer file, already with more than 2,000 records by 1995. All aspects of Maori studies are indexed. It is, however, intended as a supplement to other sources of information and therefore does not usually index material that can be easily found in library online catalogues, INNZ, *Journal of the Polynesian Society*, or the *Appendices to the Journals of the House of Representatives*. The *Bibliography* also indexes chapters or sections in books, theses and conference proceedings and some iwi newspapers. Note there is a publicity leaflet of the New Zealand Collection Librarians at Waikato University: 'The Maori Bibliography = Te Rarangi Pukapuka Maori'.

Also being kept updated and on computer file at the University of Waikato Library are: University of Waikato Library, New Zealand Collection Librarians, *Maori Biography Bibliography*, edited by Richard German; and University of Waikato Library, New Zealand Collection Librarians, *Maori Literature Bibliography*, with more than 260 records. According to the abstract in the 1993 edition of A. P. U. Millett and F. T. H. Cole, *Bibliographical Work in New Zealand ...: Work in Progress and Work Published*, it 'includes works by Maori authors, critical works, and works portraying Maori in literature'.

- *He waka eke noa: Maori Information Resources*, Wellington, 1991

provides a very comprehensive and wide-ranging list of sources relating to Maori topics. It is particularly useful for areas such as politics, for which separate bibliographies have not been compiled. It is divided into twelve sections: introduction, te reo Maori, oral arts, written arts, te mahi taonga, maoritanga, Maori women, history, the way ahead, information, management and bibliographies. Most of these general categories are further subdivided (for example the oral arts section subdivides into 'karanga', 'wahikorero', 'waiata', 'haka', 'whakatauki', 'whakapapa', 'pakiwaitara' and 'tribal and regional histories'). None of the items is annotated, but all have full bibliographic data.

- *Te Manu Aute: the paper kite, A Selective Annotated Bibliography of Maori Studies*, Wellington, 1983

is an excellent introductory bibliography on Maori topics. It is a selective bibliography but the compilers selected from a comprehensive collection of material up to 1978 and have included some readily available publications since then. The critical annotations indicate the value of items. There are two sections: 'recommended items' [Tino pai], and 'be careful' [Kia tupato] — items which are oversimplified, outdated or have other flaws which restrict their usefulness. The first section is further subdivided by topic: language, art, etc. A separate author and title index is included.

Joan Metge, *The Maoris of New Zealand*, rev. ed., London, 1976, has a bibliography which, despite its age, is still an important resource for researchers, providing one of the most comprehensive lists available of books relating to Maori. The bibliography is located at the end of the monograph. It is divided into sections with items arranged alphabetically by author: A. The Maoris before 1800; B. The Years Between; C. Maoris in the Twentieth Century; D. 1. language, 2. literature in or translated from Maori, 3. critical studies in Maori literature, 4. literature in English; E. Regional History. There are no annotations or additional indexing.

A note inside

- Cyril Mako, *A Directory of the location of statistics on the New Zealand Maori population from official sources: Putunga Tatautanga Maori*, Wellington, 1991

states that it is the 'first attempt to collect together the vast range of official statistics that are collected about the Maori population of New Zealand'. The emphasis is on regularly published statistics. Possible contacts for unpublished sources of statistics are listed. There is a subject index to the statistics available. These include statistics on age, cancer, courts, dwellings, etc. The statistics are arranged by subject. The *Directory* lists publications available, not annotated.

Other bibliographical sources include

- Jenifer Curnow, *Nga pou arahi: ko te rarangi-a-iwi o nga tuhituhinga mo nga taonga Maori, ara mo te reo, mo nga whakapapa, mo nga waiata, mo nga korero, mo nga tikanga, mo nga whakatauki = Tribal Inventory of Manuscripts relating to Maori Treasures, Language, Genealogy, Songs, History, Customs and Proverbs*, Auckland, 1995

and a computer file held at the Canterbury Museum

- Canterbury Museum and Library, *The Maori Research Index— an index of people and place names indexed from manuscript and published items.*

According to a Canterbury Museum publicity leaflet, about 1,500 people and 4,000 place names have been indexed, and as advised in the scope note in *Te Hikoi Marama: A Directory of Maori Information*

Resources [above, **10.1**] the index was prepared in conjunction with the Ngai Tahu Maori Trust Board to index 'people, places, cultural items and concepts from all types of records held at the museum and relevant to South Island Maori'.

> • University of Auckland Library, New Zealand and Pacific Collection, *Maori Writers: A Preliminary Bibliography*, compiled by E. Orwin, A. Duis and G. Dallimore, Auckland, 1984

was 'compiled in response to a request from the Pacific Information Centre, University of the South Pacific, for contributions to a projected Bibliography of Pacific Island Writers' which does not appear to have eventuated yet. All references cited are to published monographs or items in periodicals. It only includes authors who have published in the twentieth century. It is organised by author and subdivided by format within each author. It covers 89 authors and includes a checklist of writers listed. A University of Auckland internal publication, it does not seem to be widely available.

The Queen Elizabeth II Arts Council of New Zealand Resource Centre's photocopied *Nga Mea Maori: a Bibliography of Materials available from the Resource Centre*, Wellington, 1986, 'covers a wide range of materials on and relating to Maori culture with an emphasis on arts and crafts', divided by format. Although the scope is limited to the Resource Centre collection, the publication draws together an extensive collection of material relating to Maori art. There are no additional indexes, but there is a listing of subject headings used in the card catalogue and the vertical file, and alphabetical arrangement within sections. None of the items is annotated.

A Catalogue prepared by Jonathan Dennis for the New Zealand Film Archive, *He pito whakaatu a nga iwi Maori = Films of the Tangata Whenua: te Maori: te hokinga mai = the Return Home. Auckland City Art Gallery, 28 June-10 Sept. 1987*, is 'not intended to be the definitive catalogue of this material but it does include many of the more vigorous, important and moving films yet made in this country'. In the absence of a more complete listing, this catalogue is of great value to anyone researching Maori films. It includes around 60 films, which are arranged chronologically. Each item has a brief content note, title, and notes on production, photography, length and type of film used. It also includes a title index.

> • *Maori Women; An Annotated Bibliography*, by Kathie Irwin, with Michelle Erai and Lenaire Wilcox, Wellington, c1993

is a very useful source for information by or about Maori **women**. It is organised alphabetically by author with a detailed subject index. Some items are annotated. Exclusions (or areas requiring further study) included women in Maori magazines such as *Te Ao Hou, Te Kaea, Te Iwi o Aotearoa, Te Karanga*, legends, newspapers, Maori proverbs, oral histories, arts, and sport.

On **race relations** there is Leslie Smith, *Race Relations in New Zealand: a bibliography 1970-86*, Auckland, 1987. It is divided into four subject groupings: 1. general references, 2. Treaty of Waitangi references, 3. additional sources, 4. anti-racist publications sources. The scope includes published material which is generally available. The material is organised alphabetically by author within subject groupings. None of the items is annotated. A useful bibliography if beginning research in this area, although the lack of descriptors indicating value/extent of items detracts from the value.

An old work is Richard Thompson, *Race Relations in New Zealand: A Review of the Literature*, Christchurch, 1963.

For anyone interested in tribes of the **Tai Tokerau** an indispensable source is *A Catalogue of Manuscript, Printed and Published Material in the Maori Language Relating to the History and Traditions of the Tribes in Taitokerau; A Catalogue of Maori Traditions of Taitokerau Held on Tape in the Archive of Maori and Pacific Music at the University of Auckland*, compiled by Jane McRae, revised by Te Aniwaniwa Hona, Whangarei, 1989. The indexes increase the access available to this material — particularly manuscript material.

10.4.4 Maori bibliographies: land and land claims

Note 'Atlases, gazetteers and maps': 4.5

Thanks to the work of the Waitangi Tribunal in particular there has been generated an increasing number of guides to aid researchers into Maori land claims, although as a search through the New Zealand parliamentary papers show, there was always plenty of information there for those who cared to look.

There are published indexes to the New Zealand parliamentary papers — the *Appendices to the Journals of the House of Representatives* [**7.1.2**]. As well may be noted:

> 'Maori land claims as recorded in Appendices to Journals of House of Representatives and the Legislative Council from 1855-1985', Wellington, 1987; unpublished typescript, prepared by staff of the Parliamentary Library and available for purchase on microfiche.

This index does not include all Maori claims made to parliament for land, only those claimants whose petitions were tabled. The material is organised chronologically with each entry giving the claimant (individual/tribe), the claim, and unusual notes or circumstances of a claim. Claimants, iwi and regions are not indexed and to look up a particular claim or claimant it is necessary to know the year a claim was made. But at the least this list does shortcut ploughing through all the indexes and contents pages of the *Appendices*.

> *Material by Maori from the Appendices to the Journals of the House of Representatives 1860-69*, compiled by Evan Morgan and Jane Falloon, Waitangi Tribunal Occasional Paper 2, Wellington, 1993

is a paper intended to assist researchers into claims or with interest in this area by gathering the material from the *Appendices* into one volume. Most of it is in Maori, with accompanying translations. It is arranged and indexed — by people and place — chronologically by year.

Noted above [**4.5**] are the various compilations by R. P. Hargreaves, including his *Maps in the Appendices to the Journals, House of Representatives: A Chronological Listing, Part I: 1861-1890, Part II: 1891-1907*, Dunedin, 1968, a useful source for land claims, although there is no index or annotations. Each entry notes the title and date of the map with altogether 1031 titles.

Other useful indexes to land-related information include:

R. P. Hargreaves' *Maps of New Zealand Appearing in British Parliamentary Papers*, Dunedin, 1962.

(Organised chronologically, this consists of around 70 maps. It includes a subject index which has entries under 'Maoris' and is a valuable source for land claims.)

> *Turton's Land Deeds of the North Island*, microfiche edition (39 fiche)

and

> *A Compendium of Official Documents relative to Native Affairs in the South Island*, compiled by Alexander Mackay, with a new index and chronology compiled by Rohi Williams and Josie Laing in the Canterbury Museum, microfiche edition (14 fiche), both republished by the Alexander Turnbull Library, Wellington, 1991.

The Mackay documents relate to land purchases. There is a good guide to the contents of the *Compendium*. Each volume has a chronological inventory and a name/subject index, with cross-references from variants of names.

> *Summary and Index of Royal and Other Commissions concerning Maori Land Claims 1856-1975*, compiled by

Kevin Mutch, edited by Juliet McLean, Wellington, 1990
('compiled as course work for Maori Land Law, VUW,
1984, edited 1990')

names commissions' membership, indicates where information can be
found and briefly notes the issues discussed. An index of places,
statutes, concepts and broad headings is provided. The citations for the
more important commissions are quite detailed; others may only merit
a sentence. This is a useful compilation for identifying commissions
relating to specific regions and also of value for iwi-related
information.

Of late, various indexes and guides have been compiled to
legislation which is relevant to claims.

Heather Bassett, Rachel Steel and David Williams, *The Maori
Land Legislation Manual = Te puka ako hanganga mo nga
ture whenua Maori*, Wellington, 1994

was written and compiled for Crown Forestry Rental Trust and is
available in both print and electronic format. It was updated in 1995 by
*The Maori land legislation manual = Te puka ako hanganga mo nga
ture whenua Maori: volume 2* (Wellington, 1995). The contents are
drawn from a comprehensive scrutiny of all legislation enacted in New
Zealand affecting Maori or Maori land from 1840-1993. It summarises
important pieces of legislation and notes the historical context. Items
are organised chronologically.

*Customary Maori Land and Sea Tenure = Nga tikanga tiaki
taonga o nehera*, Wellington, 1991

is a bibliography of sources of information which does not include
published secondary material, but mainly consists of items taken from
primary sources. The introductory section details sources and
exclusions, the bibliographical references and the indexes. Sources
searched included evidence presented to the Waitangi Tribunal, early
minute books of the Native/Maori Land court, *Appendices to the
Journals of the House of Representatives* and older records of the
Native Department. According to the authors the bibliography is
organised by main subject categories and item number. This is not at
all clear to the casual user. In the main bibliography the subject
categories are not clearly labelled or separated. Additional access is
however provided with a detailed subject index giving cross-references
to the item number and titles as well as an iwi index.

Maori Land Legislation 1862-1908: annotations, compiled by
Tarah Nikora and Tom Bennion, Waitangi Tribunal
Occasional Publication No. 1, Wellington, 1993

is an 'aid to finding the law in force affecting Maori land transactions from 1862-1908'. Statutes and their amendments can be accessed chronologically by name, or by enactment or repeal dates. There is no separate indexing, which means the researcher must know the date of the legislation — or look through all the acts chronologically.

Intended not only for lawyers but also for planners, the public and Maori people,

> *Tai Whati: judicial decisions affecting Maoris and Maori land, 1958-1983*, Wellington, 1984

includes decisions of Maori and general courts and also references to post-1958 writings relevant to the 'law, and the Maori, and the development and administration of Maori land'. Only summaries of decisions are provided. In addition there are an alphabetical table of cases summarised in the text, an alphabetical list of index subject headings, the index itself which also incorporates references to books, theses, dissertations and articles not summarised in the text, and the case summaries in chronological order.

Tai Whati: judicial decisions affecting Maoris and Maori Land from 1958: 1984-85 supplement, Wellington, 1986, covers cases received during 1984-85 after the printing of the main text plus earlier cases omitted from the main text. It has the same index but also has a chronological listing of case summaries. *Tai Whati 1984-85 index to judicial decisions affecting Maoris and Maori land*, Wellington, 1987 is, as entitled, simply an index for the 1984-85 period, giving a table of cases summarised in the text, a listing of index subject headings and a subject index.

10.4.5 Maori bibliographies: language

Note 'Dictionaries': 4.3

Peter Ranby, *Maori Language Bibliography 1969-1979* (Working papers in Anthropology, Archaeology, Linguistics, Maori Studies, number 55), Auckland, 1980, includes writing on the teaching of Maori and the grammatical structure of the language, on the extent and nature of present knowledge of Maori and on bilingual schooling. Some manuscript items which fall outside the period are listed, as they are not known to have been included in earlier bibliographies. Works dealing with Maori literature and works of literary criticism are not included. The bibliography is organised alphabetically by author and there are no annotations or additional indexes. This is a checklist which is now in need of updating.

Richard A. Benton, compiler, *Materials for Teaching and Learning the Maori Language: a bibliography of published materials for teaching Maori to speakers of other languages*, Wellington, 1979, is separated into dictionaries and word lists, grammars, teachers' manuals, instructional materials, readers and anthologies, serials. Cross-references are made for items relevant to more than one category. Items have descriptive annotations and these indicate their level. There is a separate author index. While obviously only current up to 1980, it remains a useful guide for teachers of Maori looking for texts.

Appendix A Writing and Publication

Guides and Cautions

Guides and manuals
Format
    The bibliography
        Primary sources
        Secondary works
    Annexe: some common abbreviations

Be urgent, be patient, be painstaking — and finish the job.

    The scholar faces two tasks: first, deciding exactly what she or he is trying to do; second, setting about it in an ordered fashion, with economy of time and effort. Of the two tasks, as anyone with experience of research knows, the first is the more difficult. There are the rare writers who can produce a complete work at the first attempt without need for revision or, like the great historian Sir Lewis Namier, immerse themselves in their studies and after long gestation produce splendid results. Few, however, have such qualities, or opportunities. Many writers find that the first draft is useful for thinking their way through the material, and marks the finishing of an important stage in the work — but it is nevertheless unsatisfactory, requiring rewriting (perhaps many rewritings) and drastic cutting and rearrangement. Verbiage is a common weakness in writing up research and calls for ruthless editing of drafts. Clarity and style are the hallmarks of the good author.

Guides and manuals

There are helpful aids, not just for the beginner but also for the more experienced. For example, David Evans, a Melbourne academic, has written a modest little book, *How to Write a Better Thesis or Report*, Melbourne, 1995, in which he distils the hints and suggestions he has developed over years of advising students. He found, of course, that advice for one set of writers equally applies to all — including himself. Hence, too, a work like *Dental Writing* by F. W. Craddock, Dunedin, 1968, its value artfully disguised by its title, turns out to be an elegant little book, worth reading by anyone who thinks she or he has something to say in writing.

    The particular value of the David Evans book is that it is written by one who not only states well points which if readily known are also readily forgotten, but as a user of word processors he offers handy hints for the inexperienced — and others. Even for the experienced writer, a good guide, such as this one, will provide at least some helpful suggestion, or jog into greater awareness of what is being attempted. For the beginner, it is a work which is worth having at the elbow. (Another elbow book, of course, is a dictionary.)

David Evans is but a recent example of guides written for researchers. Among the better ones is Kate L. Turabian, *A Manual for Writers of Term Papers, Theses, and Dissertations*, 6th ed., revised by John Grossman and Alice Bennett, Chicago, 1996.

On the use of pictorial material, see A. Murray-Oliver, 'Why pictures?', *New Zealand Libraries* 32 (1969): 178-90, and Joan McCracken, 'Looking at photographs', *New Zealand Journal of Geography* 92 (1991): 12-14. There is *Picture Research: a Practical Guide*, by John and Barbara Schultz, New York, 1991, and *The Picture Researcher's Handbook: an international guide to picture sources and how to use them,* by Hilary and Mary Evans, 5th ed., London, 1992 (which has only three New Zealand references). Advice for handling oral material is given in Judith Fyfe and Hugo Manson, *Oral History and How to Approach It*, Wellington, 1991; Louise Douglas, Alan Roberts, and Ruth Thompson, *Oral History: A Handbook*, London, 1988; Trevor Lummis, *Listening to History: The Authenticity of Oral Evidence*, London, 1987; Paul Thompson, *The Voice of the Past: Oral History*, Oxford, 1978.

The New Zealand Writer's Handbook, by John Parsons, revised edition 1998, lists who (newspapers, magazines, books) publish what sort of work, as well as including chapters on tools of the trade: libraries, computers, awards and writing courses, and manuscript preparation.

When it comes to final presentation — to publisher, editor, or examiner — there are both rules and suggestions to recognise and consider. Most obviously there are rules regarding such basics as footnoting and bibliographies, not to mention grammar. But also there are conventions, for example, about capitalisation, or use of foreign terms. Even the best writers may produce sloppy or rather mindless indexes. A bit of common sense does help. Fortunately, most writers realise that short-cuts developed by medieval scribes writing with quill on parchment are not needed today, and hence have discarded the Latin abbreviations they used. Most writers, too, realise that in the English language with proper names the norm is to place the surname last, unless, and only unless, names are in an alphabetical listing as in a telephone directory or index.

A splendid and comprehensive guide on the preparation of books and articles for publication, including index preparation and how to correct proofs, is the internationally recognised *The Chicago Manual of Style*, 14th ed., Chicago, 1993. Much shorter than the *Chicago Manual* is the now out-of-print *The New Zealand Government Printing Office Style Book*, 3rd. ed., 1981. This style book began in 1958 as a manual for editors, writers and public servants preparing copy for the Government Printing Office, the now privatised and renamed (GP Publications) agency which used to handle all official publications. It can be taken to give standard New Zealand usage for punctuation, abbreviation, italicisation, capitalisation, citation. Less prescriptive, and hence not perhaps as useful, is the latest revision: *The Style Book: A Guide for New Zealand Writers and Editors*, revised by D. Wallace and J. Hughes, Wellington 1995. Journals and publishing houses have their own house styles which will vary slightly from one to the next. They will, however, provide their own style sheet to would-be authors.

The Australian equivalent to the New Zealand *Style Book*, the *Australian Government Publishing Service Press Style Manual*, now in its fifth edition, has been adapted by Lincoln University Press for New Zealanders as *Write Edit Print Style Manual for Aotearoa New Zealand*, edited by Tanya Tremewan, Canberra, 1997. This is a comprehensive attempt, as its publishers declare, to give 'principles of good writing and editing, punctuation, grammar, spelling, referencing, typesetting and printing conventions, non-discriminatory language, and publication layout'.

Another Australian guide adapted for New Zealand needs is *Getting Published*: *The Aotearoa Guide*, by Samantha Schwarz, adapted by Jenny Heine and Katherine Wellings, Wellington, 1997. As its title implies the work focuses on finding and dealing with a publisher.

Of course in tertiary institutions students can expect to be provided with some basic advice on presentation, perhaps with samples of good work. Few, however, extend as far as F. W. Craddock's *Dental Writing* for dentists, mentioned above, or (twice as long) a work for English students produced by the University of Otago: *Studying English Literature: A Guide for Advancing Students*, edited by Alistair Fox, Department of English, University of Otago, 1991. This is just as well; these works are excellent, but a student would be overwhelmed if she or he met such manuals of assistance in every subject studied.

A little problem arising for modern writers is how to cite **electronic sources**. Xia Li and Nancy Crane have produced *Electronic Styles: a handbook for citing electronic information*, 2nd ed., 1996. There are now also a number of guides available on the Internet found, for example, by searching for 'citation of Internet'. In an e-mail exchange of the Australian political science network in 1994, Tim Tenbensel, at the Australian National University, on 18 November 1994 gave for computer conferencing (— a space for discussion in which contributors 'post' items to the conference by e-mail) the following citation format: 1. name of contributor, 2. year of contribution, 3. title of topic in single quotes, 4. name of computer conference in italics (e.g. grns.oz.forum), 5. topic number and 6. response number if applicable, 7. date of posting (day/month/year), 8. name of the network (e.g Pegasus Networks). In the same exchange Ramesh Thakur, of Otago University, proffered: 'Reuter report on the *India News [Electronic] Network*, vol. 2, no. 78 (7 July 1993)'.

Format

A standard order might be:
  Title page
  Table of contents
  Lists of illustrations and maps
  List of abbreviations
  Preface and Acknowledgments [Some authors place this before
    the Contents]
  Text
  Appendices
  Endnotes
  Glossary
  Bibliography
  Index

The bibliography

A bibliography is a compendium of all the sources used by an author — ordered, precise and full. It serves both to show the foundations of the study and as a display of literature relevant to the topic. It does not, or at least should not, include miscellaneous items mentioned in the text but not relevant to the topic (such as a quotation from Shakespeare). Nor is it helpful or necessary to repeat in the bibliography bits and pieces cited in the footnotes and taken from a category of material, or a series, such as letters from a collection of manuscripts, articles in a newspaper or speeches made in parliament. It suffices to list in the bibliography the category consulted or searched: a particular manuscript collection, a newspaper over a set period of years, specified volumes of *Parliamentary Debates*.

Some — not many — published books have well laid-out bibliographies which can serve as models. One such is Elizabeth Hanson, *The Politics of Social Security*, Auckland, 1980. Another example is Barry Gustafson's *The First 50 Years: A History of the New Zealand National Party*, Auckland, 1986.

As appropriate, material customarily is divided into primary sources and secondary sources. Primary sources may be described as documents, letters, books, etc., written at the time which is being studied; secondary sources are subsequent accounts, written second-hand — hearsay works they might be called.

Primary sources

may be divided into (a) oral, (b) written but unpublished, and (c) published:

(a) **Oral** includes taped sound material.
(b) **Written** but unpublished includes:
  — official or government documents and archives
  — documents and archives of non-governmental organisations
  — non-official manuscript collections
  — personal correspondence with the author
(c) **Published** primary sources may include:
  — official: parliamentary debates, department reports, parliamentary papers, etc.
  — non-official: reports, proceedings, and other publications of non-governmental organisations
  — newspapers and journals of comment
  — pamphlets
  — published diaries and collections of letters.

The credibility of an author rests on the credibility of her or his sources. Vague gestures towards library holdings do not suffice: specific details should be given (files consulted, years or months of newspapers searched, volumes of parliamentary debates checked, and so on). With interviews, the subject of the interview, names of the interviewer and the interviewed, place and date of interview, number and length of interviews, method of recording, and the depository of the record, should all be indicated somewhere in the text, usually in the Bibliography.

Secondary works

normally are published (but may also be in manuscript or typescript). Depending on quantities in different categories of material, they may be subdivided into books, pamphlets, articles, unpublished theses, etc. (Any bibliographical information not provided in the work itself may be placed in square brackets, for example if no publication date were given on a pamphlet one might give [1999] or maybe [?1999].)

Annexe: some common abbreviations

Some common abbreviations should not be 'common' but are best discarded. They are included, here, however for convenient reference.

c., circa	about, approximately; for example, c. 1920
cf. confer,	compare with, compare with this
cit.	cited, cited by
col.	column
comp., comps	compiled by, compiler, compilers
e.g.	[*exempli gratia*] for example
ed., eds	edited by, editor, editors
et al.	[*et alia*] and others
f.	and the following page (line, entry, year)
ff.	and the following pages (lines, etc.)
ibid.	[*ibidem*] in the same place as the preceding reference
i.e.	[*id est*] that is
loc. cit.	[*loco citato*] in the place cited
MS, MSS	[*manuscriptum (-a)*] manuscript, manuscripts
op. cit.	[*opere citato*] in the work cited
p., pp.	page, pages
passim	here and there, throughout — indicates scattered references rather than continuous discussion over a sequence of pages
q.v.	[*quod vide*] which see, which should be seen
sec.	section
v., vol., vols	volume, volumes
...	indicates that words have been omitted from a quotation
....	indicates that the omitted portion includes a full point
[ ]	indicates addition of words not in the original
[sic]	indicates faithful transcription of incorrect facts, spelling, grammar, etc.

Appendix B New Zealand Copyright Law[1]

Copyright law in New Zealand is laid down in the 182-page Copyright Act 1994, along with the Copyright Regulations made under that Act. The National Library has published a *Guide to the Copyright Act ... for School Libraries*, by Richard Niven, Wellington, 1995. Briefly, in plain language, the law states:

> *Normally, copyright is vested in the author of original works, and/or the author's assignee or successor, until fifty years after the year of the author's death.*

The Act spells out the range of works which come under copyright: including **literary**, **dramatic**, **musical**, and **artistic works**, along with **sound recordings**, **films**, **broadcasts**. Under section 27 of the Act, a major exception to copyright material may be the bulk of official documentation — such as bills and acts of parliament, parliamentary debates, reports of committees and commissions, judgments of courts and tribunals. Formally, however, this exception will only come into effect after the appropriate statutory regulation has been issued. A point the layperson might miss is that copyright relates to material recorded or published: ideas and words uttered in themselves are not copyright. Hence a reporter, or an interviewer, may be the owner of material, not those persons whose words have been reported or recorded.

- No reproduction of copyright material may be made without permission of the owner of the copyright, whether reproduction be in a book, article, or unpublished thesis. These restrictions include reproduction of written and sound records, films, maps, illustrations, and works of art.
- Authors are not always the owner of copyright and even when they are not, their authorship must be acknowledged if known (or able to be found).

There are important **exceptions to the ban** on reproduction; for teaching purposes and for research, criticism and review:

---

1 Thanks to Professor R. J. Sutton of the University of Otago for advice on New Zealand copyright law.

(a) 'fair dealing' with material is permitted for private study and research
(b) 'fair dealing' is permitted for criticism or review, provided sufficient acknowledgment is made
(c) under specified conditions (section 44) multiple copying may be permitted for educational purposes
(d) a prescribed library may copy material for use for research or private study, provided that only a 'reasonable proportion' of a book or edition of a journal is copied, and provided also that any charges made are only to cover costs (— 'prescribed' libraries include the National and parliamentary libraries, libraries of educational establishments, and others listed in regulations)
(e) institutions may take out a copyright licence to cover photocopying by their staff (— since 1988 New Zealand publishers have established Copyright Licensing Ltd which will issue annual licences for a fee to institutions such as the universities; the proportion of a work which may be copied under this scheme is tightly prescribed).

In addition, there are provisions for persons with disabilities, such as regarding the making of copies in Braille (section 69).

There are also circumstances in which the flat fifty-year rule does not apply. For example, conditions may be imposed on the access to, or use made of, material, such as unpublished papers donated to a library. With sound recordings, there could actually be up to 100 years from time of recording before copyright expired (section 23); crown copyright normally lasts for 100 years (section 26).

For the researcher, effectively the Copyright Act allows the making of notes for study, including modest amount of photocopying for personal use, and quotation of extracts suitably acknowledged in a paper, book, or unpublished dissertation. The intention of the copyright law is to protect authors, not to trap scholars. But while it is unusual for anyone to take legal action under the Copyright Act against use of material in an unpublished thesis, research students as much as other writers should be aware of the risks to themselves of breaching copyright.

Where manuscripts are in private hands, the owner may lay down their own restrictions as to their use, and it is advisable to obtain their permission before material is reproduced. In all cases of doubt with manuscripts, the permission of the owner of the copyright should be sought and in special circumstances it may even be advisable to seek legal advice. It is important to note that the owner of the copyright may not be the same person as the owner of the manuscripts.

New Zealand copyright law is as stringent as that of most other countries, so that even in the case of publishing overseas (for example in a journal) and hence coming under another country's copyright laws, compliance with the New Zealand law will normally avoid any legal complications.

Finally, quite apart from restrictions under copyright law, special care should be taken in using information, or making comments, which might be taken to damage the reputation of a person. (Even after the expiry of copyright those affected may have rights quite apart from rights under the Copyright Act; moreover some people live long after we thought they were dead!) And, a further caution: disrespect towards cultural objects of the New Zealand indigenous people, especially digitisation of images, raises issues of custody and ongoing cultural rights extending beyond the limits of copyright law. Disrespect towards revered objects of any culture, of course, is not going to win friends.

Index

134